Messy Discipleship

The Bible Reading Fellowship
15 The Chambers, Vineyard
Abingdon OX14 3FE
brf.org.uk

The Bible Reading Fellowship (BRF) is a Registered Charity (233280)
Messy Church® is a registered trade mark of BRF

ISBN 978 0 85746 953 3
First published 2021
10 9 8 7 6 5 4 3 2 1 0
All rights reserved

Acknowledgements
Unless otherwise acknowledged, scripture quotations are taken from The Holy
Bible, New International Version (Anglicised edition) copyright © 1979, 1984, 2011
by Biblica. Used by permission of Hodder & Stoughton Publishers, a Hachette
UK company. All rights reserved. 'NIV' is a registered trademark of Biblica. UK
trademark number 1448790.

Scripture quotations marked ERV are taken from the Easy-to-Read Version,
copyright © 2006 by Bible League International. • Scripture quotations marked
MSG are taken from The Message, copyright © 1993, 1994, 1995, 1996, 2000, 2001,
2002 by Eugene H. Peterson. Used by permission of NavPress. All rights reserved.
Represented by Tyndale House Publishers, Inc. • Scripture quotations marked
NLT are taken from the Holy Bible, New Living Translation, copyright © 1996,
2004, 2007, 2013. Used by permission of Tyndale House Publishers, Inc., Carol
Stream, Illinois 60188. All rights reserved. • Scripture quotations marked NABRE
are taken from he New American Bible, revised edition © 2010, 1991, 1986, 1970
Confraternity of Christian Doctrine, Inc., Washington, DC. All Rights Reserved. •
Scripture quotations marked NRSV are taken from The New Revised Standard
Version of the Bible, Anglicised edition, copyright © 1989, 1995 by the Division of
Christian Education of the National Council of the Churches of Christ in the United
States of America. Used by permission. All rights reserved.

Every effort has been made to trace and contact copyright owners for material
used in this resource. We apologise for any inadvertent omissions or errors, and
would ask those concerned to contact us so that full acknowledgement can be
made in the future.

A catalogue record for this book is available from the British Library

Printed and bound by CPI Group (UK) Ltd, Croydon CR0 4YY

Messy Discipleship

Messy Church perspectives on growing faith

Edited by Lucy Moore

Contents

Introduction

Lucy Moore

 Lucy Moore is the founder of Messy Church. She promotes Messy Church nationally and internationally through training and speaking events, and is the author of a number of books for BRF.

The last Messy Discipleship book was published in 2013 – *Making Disciples in Messy Church* by Paul Moore. 2013! It feels like a lifetime ago. So much has changed since then: governments, step-change politics, awareness around climate change and single-use plastics, the Black Lives Matter movement, to name but a few examples. There is also a growing understanding of 'church' as something which we live out in our lives 24/7, at home, work, school or leisure activities. In the church, opinion is arguably more polarised than back in 2013 around questions of inclusion and expensive church-growth strategies, while church attendance figures in the west continue to decline in most denominations. Then, of course, in 2020, Covid-19 stampeded across everyone's lives, disturbing, disrupting, destroying, like an opened crate of velociraptors from *Jurassic Park*. Nothing will be the same in the UK. This savage rewilding has opened up spaces in the landscape of society and of church that are still at the stage of being comparatively trampled and empty, as I write. One fear is that in the church world, we will rush to replant what we want to fill these spaces rather than having the discipline and faith to watch and wait for the Holy Spirit to give a more diverse, perhaps less controlled, range of organisms the chance to take root.

What doesn't seem to have changed since 2013 in the church world are the two points over which overworked Messy Church practitioners bang their heads against the nearest wall: the first being that the biblical principle of being an all-age church is still valued by very few churches. The perfect service for the vast majority is still a nostalgic dream of 'Send the kids out to Sunday School while we adults (and one or two "nice" children, sitting "nicely") get on with proper church. We do not need to change the way we do church.' And churches are emptying, with families with children driving away from their local church to the one in the city where they have large, professionally run children's and youth groups. Chris Barnett's chapter on the all-age value of Messy Church is a timely reminder that there is still so much to do to bring disciples *together* across all divides, and that real discipleship means walking the walk with all sorts of disciples *who are different from us*.

The other head-banging point is that Messy Church is still often done 'to get people to come to proper church on a Sunday morning at 10.30 in a pew'. Only today, Matt Finch from the Methodist Church wrote to me: 'We are celebrating the numbers of Messy Churches that have sprung up, but we are wanting to support their development into ecclesial communities in their own right. At the moment there is too much of an expectation for people thriving in Messy settings to one day move to the "established" setting and sit quietly.' Claire Dalpra rightly celebrates the outreach Messy Churches. And it is certainly better to do an occasional Messy event than no sort of mission at all. But there is a fear that never moving beyond this model is self-limiting, self-satisfied and ultimately self-defeating. It will make little in the way of mature disciples because it expects little transformation. The chapters in this book on creativity, celebration, hospitality and being Christ-centred give inspiration that may well instil a holy dissatisfaction with anything less than the best we can offer our communities.

What's changed since 2013 for Messy Church specifically? Two international conferences have taken place, bringing together Messy leaders from many of the 30 countries in which it happens and growing lasting friendships between people across thousands of miles. The third conference in 2022 is being planned, not by three BRF team members, as was the first one in 2016, but by an international, multidenominational

team aged 13 upwards: we're on the way to becoming more intentionally 'mutual'. Messy Church has grown in different ways in different
countries, with varied contextual governance, including indigenous
languages for the name, such as Kliederkerk in the Netherlands and
Kirche Kunterbunt in Germany. The structure for the support of Messy
Church 'centrally' at BRF has changed from three full-time staff members (with BRF admin, publishing and web support) to an even smaller
central team and a reimagined support structure for the many UK volunteers. Since 2013 the Messy world has been immeasurably enriched
by the arrival of the Holy Habits approach to living the Christian life.

In local churches for a while, Covid-19 devastated much of what makes
Messy Church worth doing: the closeness, friendship, food, sharing,
community, unconditional welcome, participation and freedom from
authoritarianism that are so attractive to households outside the
church. But it also drove us into new ways of being hospitable, creative, finding celebration in the midst of anxiety, being Christ-centred
and appreciative of the gifts of old and young. The first steps were
made towards young Messy leaders developing their own international
leadership community with support from the network. The network
made a regular time each week to gather online in the Wednesday
Facebook Live sessions, forming a different sort of togetherness. We
created versions of the resources to be 'Messy Church at home'; shared
out 'Messy Church in a bag' by the thousands. Messy leaders joined in
the Messy Adventure for Ascension Day, travelling the world via Messy
Church videos; invented a combo of Messy Church and Minecraft for
online Bible study; created study groups based on Holy Habits for team
members; did pastoral care by text and phone; and presented a mil-
lion and one Messy sessions online. The creativity in evidence in Messy
Churches large and small, the value that Sandy Brodine explores in her
chapter, is living proof of the Holy Spirit at work, even in lockdown.

Another set of significant changes is that of the everyday lives of the
people within the movement. Any one month brings us up against
the reality of the messiness of life for the people who are the movers
and shakers of Messy Church, let alone the families who are members:

babies are born, loved ones die, critical illness takes over out of the blue, house moves disrupt, redundancy rattles certainties, retirement looms, a new calling shifts the bedrock of a life. The network reflects the incredibly transitional, ever-changing nature of family life, where a single year can transform a household unit into something unrecognisable, with the addition of a few teenage hormones or a change of job, school or relationship. The network is forever adapting, changing and, in fact, living. Is life something to celebrate or to endure? The light-touch and easily dismantled and reformed structure of Messy Church means the network can stay alive, like a hermit crab swapping shells as it changes shape.

And what hasn't changed in the world of Messy Church since 2013 is the lack of a quick-fix, flick-the-switch answer to making disciples. It remains… messy. And yet. *And yet* there are more and more guiding lights to help us take even more than the Messy team and more than the Messy movement on the journey. The problem is that those lights illuminate some paths that are so difficult that not many feel able to set out on them. Who's prepared to abandon their Sunday congregation in order to invest entirely in their Messy Church? Who has the courage to be a vulnerable and pastoral friend or surrogate family member, week in, week out? Who can make do with no recognition, encouragement or affirmation from their denominational gatekeepers? Who has time to host smaller weekly gatherings online or face to face, to build up individuals and be built up by them? There are plenty of neat theories about how a Messy Church should develop: the plain reality is that, in comparison with some forms of church that have full-time, trained, professional leaders, Messy Church is run mostly by lay people with many other commitments – including demanding commitments to inherited church. As a Messy Church leader myself, being told by experts that I must push on to the next step, move people on, add extra meetings to my week, get people on to courses, demonstrate something concrete that can be measured, leaves me – depending on my state of resilience that day – snorting at the absurdity, weeping in a slough of inadequacy or raging at the heartlessness that tries to push me and my lovely, messy, unpredictable, shifting, enquiring, edgy congregation into a tidy box where we can be counted.

In this book, we had hoped to bring you the conclusions of an exciting research project with the Church of England Deepening Discipleship in Messy Church, but Covid-19 altered the timeframe. To whet the appetite, I'll just say that we are exploring together what impact on discipleship there is if a Messy team intentionally and reflectively tries to grow disciples through one of six approaches designed to benefit either the team members or the families who belong to the Messy Church. The early results are very encouraging. But it feels as if God may be trying to say something about the essential untidy nature of life and that God's kingdom is one in which disruption is going to happen: we can either give up as the cataclysm changes the landscape around us or use the Messy values and the emerging skills of reflective practice to discover ways forward. Success isn't measured by producing a book on discipleship; success is about navigating a route through the chaos together. Like Psalm 23, what matters is that the journey is walked *together* through the valley of the shadow of death, rather than counting how many people sit down at the banquet of the king.

What has this overview got to do with discipleship? Well, the longer I spend marvelling at the goings-on in the world of Messy Church, the more I'm convinced that discipleship has less to do with a single glamorous or feel-good experience and much more to do with obedience, attitude, under-the-surface 'heart' stuff, perseverance, resilience, dogged determination, single-minded (bloody-minded, even) unstoppableness in a journey towards, with and from Jesus. ('From' because it all starts with him.) As a network, we're stumbling together in roughly the same direction throughout the years, picking up new friends on the way, listening to Jesus together, pointing out to each other where we think he's directing us, being shaped into a movement through which Jesus can grow his kingdom: that journey in itself is discipleship. Like any group of hikers on a walk, discipleship comes down to not giving up, even when there are steep mountains, discomfort, blisters, confusion, darkness and mistakes in navigation. And when your companions drive you bananas with frustration (and you realise you've been driving them equally bananas, but they've hidden it better), *even then*, you keep on believing in your purpose, your destination, the means of travel and your company. If you're not committed, you'll drop out, because what's the point of all the grief if you don't believe the journey's leading anywhere, that these are worthwhile companions, that your guide is with you every step of the way or that this is the best route?

And what's been happening over the last decade or two is a proving of the pudding that Messy Church *as a movement* is modelling a little of what discipleship is all about. It's becoming (and that 'becoming' is in itself significant, isn't it?) more confident (some would say arrogant). It's about being small, light of foot and decentralised. It's about rejoicing in the local and specific, valuing the tiny moments, celebrating the love of the amateur, being vulnerable together, laughing a lot, crying a lot, building friendship rather than rules and holding lightly rather than tightly, all in faith that our role is simply to create the welcoming space and that the Holy Spirit will do the work. In a way, it's being a metaphor for individual discipleship. It depends on community, togetherness, household, *oikos.* It has the stickability, resilience and adaptability that faces crises and, rather than giving up when it's all too hard, falls back on the strength of Christ and the strength of others, finding a way through and maybe becoming stronger through the experience, like Paul and the early church pioneers:

> And we boast in the hope of the glory of God. Not only so, but we also glory in our sufferings, because we know that suffering produces perseverance; perseverance, character; and character, hope. And hope does not put us to shame, because God's love has been poured out into our hearts through the Holy Spirit, who has been given to us.
> ROMANS 5:2–5

Character, hope and love in abundance: there is plenty of each of these in the Messy movement. And it's a movement that many of us are deeply proud and continually humbled to belong to.

Part I

How Messy Churches are enabling discipleship

Claire Dalpra

 Claire Dalpra has worked for Church Army's Research Unit since 1999, where she also trains new evangelists and leads the internal review process. Alongside this, she undertakes external research work for clients, including *Playfully Serious* and the Deepening Discipleship in Messy Church project. Claire lives in Sheffield with her husband and teenage daughter, helping to lead children and families work in an inner-city parish.

1
A researcher's journey

*Evaluating the terrain – walking alongside participants –
listening and learning*

The starting point

The four chapters of this section tell the story of *Playfully Serious*.[1] As
I write now, it is three years since I began that research journey. Our
team, Church Army's Research Unit, had not long completed *The Day
of Small Things: An analysis of fresh expressions of church in 21 dioceses*,
and we were wondering where we should turn our energies to next.
Feeling that strange combination of excited anticipation and mild ter-
ror that so often characterises the early stages of research, we began
on what eventually became *Playfully Serious* – not knowing where it
would take us.

Under the direction of Dr George Lings, Church Army's Research Unit
has been discerning the evolving mission of the church in the UK and
the phenomenon of fresh expressions of church since 1997. In *The
Day of Small Things*, we rigorously sifted mission initiatives in half the
dioceses of the Church of England according to our ten definitional
indicators, catalogued them and mathematically analysed them.

If the approach we used in *The Day of Small Things* reads as rather cold
and clinical, please know that our data collection method involved

speaking to clergy and lay leaders on the telephone. We are extremely grateful to them. As you probably already know, Messy Church was the single most common type of fresh expression of church, reported at 32.5% – that is; over six times the average 5% type reported.[2] Moreover, this is after we *excluded* more than half the Messy Churches we were given by dioceses to potentially include. The sifting process meant we researched only those Messy Churches that met the ten definitional indicators for being fresh expressions of church (fxC).[3] At times, this felt a little hard-nosed, but it was necessary to be consistent with our research definitions.

There is something intriguing about the modest approach of Messy Church being the clear front runner in the most frequently reported type of fresh expression of church. By modest, I mean it is not an approach that is particularly novel or groundbreaking. When the Church Commissioners invited us to look specifically at Anglican Messy Churches in greater depth, how could we say no?

I was asked to lead this project from its inception, within the research dimension of the variety of roles Church Army employs me to do alongside review work and teaching. I had the amazing help and support of the rest of the team, although it just so happened that the original colleagues I started with weren't the ones I finished with. I only mention this as it strikes me as rather an apt parallel; leading part-time with a changeable team sounds like the dynamics that busy Messy Church leaders have no choice but to make the best of all the time.

As a researcher with a long-standing interest in children's spirituality, I was glad to embark upon this research journey. As a parent and a practitioner, leading initiatives for children and families in a deprived inner-city Sheffield parish, it has been incredibly engaging. In these chapters, I have aimed to tell the story of this research from both a professional and personal perspective, in order to complement the formal accounts that already exist. I hope I have achieved a helpful balance of both perspectives.

The stopping point: a statistical summary

By 2019, *Playfully Serious* was finally complete and launched in February of that year. After an exasperating but worthwhile process of condensing two years of research into a mere handful of sound bites and headlines, findings were published in a colourful, glossy booklet. This was a deliberate choice of Church Army's Research Unit to serve busy Messy Church leaders, clergy, PCCs and permission-givers, putting something easy-to-read into their hands to encourage more strategic conversations. PDFs of the detailed reports were made available online for those who wished to delve more deeply into our findings.

As agreed in the contracting process, there were two overarching strands of enquiry in *Playfully Serious*. **First, how are Messy Churches enabling discipleship? Second, how are Messy Churches maturing as church?** Unlike previous research, we asked these questions to a broader range of Messy Church initiatives. We were interested in learning not only from Messy Churches that were fresh expressions of church, but also from those that were something else. It was lovely to be able to celebrate the life of outreach Messy Church initiatives who do not feel they are called to be fresh expressions of church in their contexts.

Within the life of our team, this research became something of a benchmark as the first major project to incorporate different kinds of methods. From early on, we knew we would need statistical data to capture the breadth and scope of Messy Church at a national level, but we would also need some qualitative – more in-depth – work with leaders and families to help us get under the skin of the day-to-day reality of Messy Church life.

If I introduce the different components of our research here, not only will you know the PDFs that are available, but it will also help make sense as you navigate the following chapters where I highlight key findings. For those of you who enjoy scrutinising statistics, *Painting with Numbers* is the report by Fiona Tweedie analysing 174 Messy Churches of both kinds across 21 dioceses in the Church of England.[4]

Half of the 174 were a random stratified sample of Messy Churches we included as fresh expressions of church in *The Day of Small Things*. These we ended up referring to as 'fxC MES'. The other half were a random stratified sample of Messy Churches we spoke to but did not include as fresh expressions of church as they fell outside our ten indicators. These we called 'outreach MES' for short. Created by my colleague Elspeth McGann, this relatively modest-sized sample of both types was our way of capturing a snapshot of the breadth of activity in England. Some of the significant differences reported from the two types will be further explored in chapter 4, 'A Messy Church's journey'.

This meant that all Messy Churches in our sample began before 2016[5] and had been running long enough to be logged on a diocesan list or self-registered by leaders on the Messy Church website. Our thanks to leaders who gave their time to work through quite a complex set of questions with our interviewers on the phone. This data collection also enabled us to ask some basic questions regarding frequency and days and times of meeting to understand some of the general trends, such as those reported here.[6]

There is more variety here to challenge the stereotype that Messy Church is always a monthly gathering on a weekday after school. The outreach MES percentages suggest gatherings are more than occasional gestures by churches squeezing in the odd mission event as and when they can; indeed, they show an ongoing commitment to reach out to local families.

Frequency	Total	FxC MES	Outreach MES
Occasional	4%	0%	8%
4–6 times a year	24%	1%	48%
Monthly (or nearly monthly)	67%	92%	42%
More often than monthly	5%	7%	1%

Table 1. Meeting frequencies of Messy Churches in our sample

	All MES	FxC MES	Outreach MES
Weekdays	43%	50%	36%
Saturday	31%	18%	44%
Sunday	26%	34%	19%

Table 2. Days on which Messy Churches met in our sample

	All MES	FxC MES	Outreach MES
Breakfast	0%	0%	0%
Morning	15%	10%	20%
Lunchtime	2%	0%	5%
Afternoon	17%	15%	20%
After school	26%	31%	22%
Teatime	39%	45%	33%

Table 3. Times of day at which Messy Churches met in our sample

The stopping point: findings from interviews

Managing the Mess[7] is our report of the focus group interviews we conducted with 29 Messy Church leaders across different parts of England, asking questions around both strands of discipleship and church maturity. I am indebted to five Regional Coordinators for assisting me in hosting these interviews and providing cake to share as leaders reflected together. *Managing the Mess* is a summary of the coding my colleague Isaac Stovell applied to the vast amount of data we gathered – teasing out what leaders are proactive about, at the same time as their impressions of how what happens is received by attenders. By proactive, I refer to those actions a leader can take to try to model values, encourage faith conversations and build a sense of community – knowing that how attenders respond is not always something they can control.

What Goes On Inside[8] is our short report on our research with attenders – parents and children. This was the first time our team had embarked on research with children and the first time we incorporated creative research methods into a larger project. Research so often draws on the opinions of leaders only. Here we wanted to include the voices of families, especially children. We collected both verbal and non-verbal data by inviting them to create a piece of artwork as a response to our questions as a way into interview. Our thanks to all those who took part for their willingness to engage in what must have felt like a slightly strange mix of research and fun.

Other research outputs[9] included analysis of some telephone interviews with families who had stopped coming to Messy Church after regularly attending, and further analysis of those 49 Messy Churches in our sample of 174 which had since closed. We are especially appreciative of leaders and attenders for whom Messy Church is no longer a feature of their present season of life. Having to answer questions about a current initiative over the phone is laborious enough; in the busyness of life, to have to answer for an initiative that closed some years ago might have felt like mild torture.

The point of not knowing

Working for Church Army, with its 150 years of selecting, training and deploying evangelists to work for the Anglican Church in the British Isles, conversations around where evangelism ends and discipleship begins are familiar ground. Furthermore, Church Army serves the whole breadth of churchmanship found within the Anglican Church. We are well aware of the different closely held convictions of what is important regarding discipleship within different church traditions.

However, this still did not prepare us for the challenges this research presented in defining discipleship and how to go about measuring it. As a team, we embarked on a discipleship literature review at the beginning of the research process and were considerably boggled by the diverse understandings of this single word bandied about so easily by us and others in the wider church. At my lowest point in the research journey, I felt I was trying to measure something immeasurable and could not see a way forward through all the complexity.

Reflecting on this existing literature on discipleship, albeit a relatively modest sample, eventually led to something of a breakthrough. To hold together different perspectives, I created a framework to balance various apparently contradictory dynamics:

- formal learning and informal learning
- key moments of decision and lifelong journey
- head knowledge and heart response
- owned individually and owned in relationship
- inner transformation and outer transformation.

A paper unpacking these dynamics called *Discipleship Definitions* is one of our supplementary research outputs for anyone who would like to read it.[10]

It is curiously unfair that Messy Churches are sometimes closely scrutinised for evidence of discipleship in ways that existing forms of churchgoing or other mission models do not seem to be. Perhaps it is inevitable that when something in church life proves wildly popular, harder questions are then asked to prove it has merit and isn't just a fad.

Like *The Day of Small Things*, this *Playfully Serious* research took the opportunity to ask leaders to estimate the church backgrounds of attenders, including their team. A relatively high percentage of de-churched and non-churched were reported across the 174 Messy Churches in our sample – with only 38% thought to be existing churchgoers.[11]

	Churched	De-churched	Non-churched
All MES	38%	21%	40%
FxC MES	37%	22%	41%
Outreach MES	40%	20%	40%

Table 4. Leaders' perception of the proportion of attenders by previous church involvement

Interestingly, there is little difference in the proportions perceived in fxC MES and those in outreach MES. While acknowledging this as only a *perception* of reality, and that these simple terms can't really do justice to the complicated life and faith experience of individuals, Messy Churches still report greater non-churched percentages than most other types of fresh expression of church.[12] What Messy Churches have the courage to learn in their discipleship of this mix of attenders will help us all with our rapidly growing mission field of so many who have never had any meaningful contact with church and have 'no knowledge of the Bible at all'.[13]

Unlike *The Day of Small Things*, this research tracked the type of context Messy Churches were located in via postcode. Approximately one-third (34%) of our sample of Messy Churches served rural areas; two-thirds served urban locations. It also contained a remarkably even spread of Messy Churches across areas of different economic deprivation as described by the Index of Multiple Deprivation (IMD).[14] Overall, we found bewilderingly little significant statistical difference between the findings reported by the most deprived (decile 1 or 2) and the least deprived (decile 9 or 10). Again, what Messy Churches have the courage to learn in more deprived areas now will help us all in the future – especially in areas where the Church of England has historically struggled to see ministry flourish.

Location	% of all MES	FxC MES	Outreach MES
Urban locations	66%	68%	63%
Rural locations	34%	32%	37%
Deprivation quintile	% of all MES	FxC MES	Outreach MES
Decile 1 or 2	21%	19%	22%
Decile 3 or 4	18%	21%	15%
Decile 5 or 6	21%	17%	26%
Decile 7 or 8	18%	21%	15%
Decile 9 or 10	22%	23%	22%

Table 5. The social context of Messy Churches using deprivation indices

I still believe discipleship should remain something of a mystery. The fact that something so life-giving was taking me – in terms of how I felt emotionally – to such a dark place and was a difficult concept to measure reminded me of Peck's observation that some things are bigger and more mysterious than we can humanly pin down.[15] These indefinable concepts, such as love and community, can't be contrived or controlled. All that you can do is create environments in which they are more likely to thrive.

The idea that, at the very least, we can create environments in which discipleship might thrive kept me going. Rather than enforce a kind of ivory-tower definition, we used our different methods of research to continue to discern what resonated with Messy Church leaders and attenders themselves. Our research showed us that others, too, were confused. 'What do you mean by discipleship?' was sometimes asked of us during our telephone interviews. Anecdotally, some talked of discipleship of newcomers as the thing the vicar took care of. Or they wanted to help with discipleship, but they didn't want to do the wrong thing.

At a basic level, Messy Church already has teaching about worship, prayer and the Bible woven firmly into its model; as a leader commented in our focus group interviews, the group 'kind of accepts that you're going to talk like that in the celebration time'.[16] For families who have had little or no connection with church before, we should not pass too quickly over reported engagement with the Bible.[17] The statistics confirm that craft and storytelling as part of the celebration are relatively 'normal' for both types of Messy Church; additional ways of encouraging families to engage with the Bible appear to be happening slightly more in the fresh expressions of church sample.

	Storytelling	Creative activity/ resource	Talk	Take home activity for families	Passages read in public	Memory verses	Encourage individual reading at home	Study in groups
All MES	96%	95%	70%	32%	31%	12%	9%	5%
FxC MES	98%	98%	75%	32%	39%	16%	13%	10%
Outreach MES	94%	93%	64%	31%	23%	8%	6%	2%

Table 6. Engagement with the Bible at Messy Church

At the same time, we also asked about progress in helping attenders learn to pray.[18] Again, this question was asked in a fairly simple way with no deeper enquiry as to whether this was joining in with public prayers, praying out loud on one's own or praying in private. Also, the question did not differentiate between adults and children. It was based very much on a leader's gut feeling from what they were able to observe of – or hear about from – attenders. For fxC MES, 'some' progress was reported by the biggest number of MES, while for outreach MES, the responses were centred around 'a little' progress.

What progress is being made on helping attenders to learn to pray?					
	None	A little	Some	A lot	Don't know
All MES	9%	34%	36%	10%	11%
FxC MES	5%	27%	47%	14%	8%
Outreach MES	13%	42%	24%	6%	15%

Table 7. Learning to pray at Messy Church

When we asked about the ways they measure discipleship, some said they thought they saw evidence of deeper discipleship but in ways that we have not traditionally measured it. The most common answer was the transformation of character, chosen by over half of the leaders (58%), followed by using and discovering gifts in ministry (47%). When asked about the hurdles or barriers to developing discipleship further, leaders selected 'team too busy' (60%) and 'families not ready' (56%) as their best guesses as to why it can be so hard.[19]

Over the hard part

Writers such as Roxburgh[20] and Arbuckle[21] encourage us to see the times of darkness and unknowing as necessary times when God does something new through our letting go of control. The way forward for our methodology did slowly emerge, spurred on by having to give families participating in the attenders' research – subsequently called *What Goes On Inside* – enough of an idea of what discipleship was by way of stimulus. We realised that to invite them to reflect on their discipleship in Messy Church without any introduction or definitional framework would have been very difficult for them.

Having sat with the statistical data and coded focus group interviews, we discerned that the analogy of journey was one already used by a few Messy Churches. In our research with families, we explained discipleship as 'a journey of following Jesus throughout the whole of your life'. What seemed a little simplistic at first settled with us as the most helpful explanation that we had come across.

The image of a journey may be somewhat clichéd these days, but it paints a helpful image of the spiritual life as an ever-evolving one (never static). A journey has linear elements but also includes short-cuts, U-turns and going round in circles that go some way to symbol-ise life's unpredictability. 'Journey' picks up on the poetic imagery in scripture of hard paths, which include the valley of the shadow of death in Psalm 23 as well as the promise of straightened paths for followers in Proverbs 3, and not forgetting the traditional Irish prayer asking that roads rise up to meet us as we pray for blessing.

The analogy of journey leaves room for that combination of individual endeavour and communal companionship as we seek to follow Jesus with others. As the next chapter explores, Messy Church's focus on children and families naturally invites exploration with one another, perhaps unlike the individual internal engagement of adult-only worship or private devotion. Journey offers that outward and inward experience of both physical effort and spiritual contemplation. Lastly, it may seem trite to some, but I am always surprised by how accessible and deeply touching the famous 'Footsteps' poem is – even to those new to church. The idea that someone or something might be carrying you through difficult times, even though you may not realise it at the time, seems to resonate with a lot of people.

We learned from our research with attenders in *What Goes On Inside* that there are ways to encourage people to talk about the things we don't see – the inner world of belief and spirituality. We also learned that it is likely to happen most when people can use a combination of verbal and non-verbal communication methods. Pointing out the obvious, we make the most of symbol in the normal course of church life to explain the deep mysteries of our faith. When words seem inadequate, we use the imagery of water, oil, ash, candles, liturgical colour and, of course, bread and wine (and so much more) to express something deeper.

Paint, collage work and clay were the ways in which we found our research conversations began to open up, but these are not the only way by any means. What mattered was having *time* in this research to think about the way we felt confident to explain discipleship to our attenders in creative ways that they would understand, especially children, but also adults unfamiliar with the language and culture of church.

At a workshop at the 2019 Messy Church international conference, I gave a group of Messy Church leaders time to create their own visual way of explaining discipleship that was appropriate for them, their teams and their attenders to stimulate discussion. Some amazing examples emerged. These included someone using real (not drawings of) leaves, blossom and bark, another creating a hand-drawn map and one creating their own backpack, to use as analogies for conversation with families.

In doing this, I felt we were glimpsing treasure, like different facets of a diamond, drawing encouragement – rather than disappointment – from only being able to know the mystery of discipleship in part. The sense of positivity, fun and creativity from all those who have participated and interacted with this research has been an unexpectedly beautiful and hope-filled sunrise on my journey.

Questions to consider

1 If you are unsure where to go next with your Messy Church, don't panic. Take heart that this can be a liminal (between) space of relinquishing control and asking for God's wisdom in discerning the right way forward. What wisdom or guidance do you need for the next part of the journey? Pray for it. Share your feelings with someone who will listen and pray with you to discern the right way forward.

2 Have you found a short, creative way to explain discipleship to your Messy Church families? If not, why not have a go at designing something that suits you and your context? Try it out with your team.

3 What will help your families to explore and reflect even more what is going on inside for them spiritually? Will art be the starting point or will some other non-verbal way work better for your Messy Church?

2

An attender's journey

*Following the path – running ahead or lagging behind –
enjoying the view*

The next three chapters continue to explain the *Playfully Serious*
findings. What follows tackles some concepts that are as equally
big as 'discipleship' and 'journey' – loaded words, such as 'family',
'leadership', 'church' and 'catholicity', which require some unpacking. We start with what we discovered from listening to our Messy
Church attenders. In our sample, we found 8,076 people, of whom
47% were adults (16- and 17-year-olds were counted as adults), 5%
were 12–15-year-olds and 49% were children.[22] One of the ongoing
challenges with any children and families ministry is maintaining a
balance of attention to how children are growing in their faith as well
as the teenagers and adults who attend. Beginning with the children,
what did we learn about the different age groups in this research?

The journey of a child

Incorporating the voice of children in this research – even a small
sample – was a priority from early on. To not represent them as key
stakeholders felt wrong. For sociological researchers, involving children and young people as participants within – or indeed co-creators
of – research is entirely normal.[23] In the world of the church, we're nov-
ices at this. On the whole, we're right to remain cautious due to ethical

considerations. Academic and theological institutions have rigorous ethics checklists and panel approval for this kind of research.[24] However, at the same time we must take care to avoid general judgements about the effectiveness of an initiative for the family from an adult perspective only.

How are we to understand the term 'family' in this day and age? Is it those who live under the same roof as you? Those you are related to by blood? Those you spend time with outside work and school? Knowing that families come in all shapes and sizes, we listened to the individual perspectives of 30 children and adults, rather than trying to conduct some sort of collective family interview process. We designed our research so that children were always with their adult family member in the same room; not only did that simplify our approach, but it was a lovely way to conduct the research in the spirit of the Messy Church all-age value.

My reading around children's spirituality and the theology of childhood alerted me early on to the different way Jesus interacted with children. Whereas with adults Jesus' conversation involved a challenge, forgiveness and change of behaviour, with children he welcomed them just as they were.[25] This is modelled in the choice of stories in the curriculum used by Godly Play to nurture Christian spiritually in children's lives. Encountering Jesus is about unconditional blessing, which is why welcoming children into church life is so crucial.[26] While devotees of Messy Church and advocates of Godly Play are usually quick to emphasise the differences that exist within these two approaches, I rejoice in the wonderful similarity that I see in both. In their different ways, they are extremely good at offering children unconditional blessing.

We valued the thoughtful comments made by the children in our interviews, including the following:

> I'm painting a forest… the journey through things… My craft is about the journey of being faithful to God… like you're walking

through a forest and you're camping out for the night.
Panda, aged 9

If people don't really know Jesus or they don't follow him, it's a sign to say about Jesus and if you want you can follow him.
Candy, aged 9

We talked about growth and journeying with Jesus and continuing that journey was the leaves, wasn't it?
    Yeah. And then the blossom is they have a deep relationship with Jesus.
Ruth, adult, and Rebecca, aged 11[27]

Some writers go further and conclude that, rather than empty vessels to be filled with knowledge about the Christian faith, there is, as Wordsworth wrote, something of 'heaven that lies about us in our infancy'.[28] Discipleship in childhood is more about facilitating regular opportunities for children to explore their own spirituality – much like spiritual retreat – that become normal as they grow into adulthood. And we shouldn't be afraid to touch upon the more difficult aspects of life and faith – rather than sugar-coating the Bible's teaching – so they are not thrown by life's 'curve balls' when they are older.[29]

Before my reflections get too worthy or noble or idealistic, I will note that ministry among children can be wonderfully chaotic. Some sessions never quite work as you expect them to. Either there is a disruptive toddler who won't settle or a child who will insist on burying their favourite dinosaur toy in the sand in which you are trying to tell the story of Moses and the ten commandments.

Personally, I never begrudge the seemingly random, even when a child is telling you about a television programme they watched with zombies in it. It is what is currently in the forefront of their minds and to listen well to them is part of the blessing we can offer. Occasionally, there are the special times, such as when you realise a child likening the story of Saul escaping Damascus over the wall in a basket to the film *Titanic* isn't random; it's the child understanding – from watching the film 25 times – how scared Saul was, because they know what Rose was feeling in the lifeboat.

I suspect I'm preaching to the converted here. In the Church of England, 65.3% of our churches reported fewer than five children or young people under the age of 16 on a Sunday, so I'm delighted that so many children will experience unconditional welcome in church through Messy Church.[30] For them to participate in something fun, with the freedom to ask all their relevant and random questions: what will this sow and reap in years to come, I wonder? Research conducted by ComRes for the Church of England discovered that 40% of Christians interviewed said they came to faith as young children under the age of five.[31] We underestimate the spiritual significance of these early years of life at our peril.

The child baptism and confirmation statistics are a helpful benchmark to discipleship among children – as two key moments of decision on one's faith journey. Findings within our sample of 174 reported in *Painting with Numbers* included the following:[32]

Baptisms	In Messy Church	Messy Church but another time	Sunday morning congregation
All MES	14%	7%	50%
FxC MES	21%	13%	47%
Outreach MES	8%	1%	54%

Table 8. Where Messy Church members are being baptised

The 'Messy Church but another time' category refers to those baptisms conducted with the usual Messy Church families attending but on a different day, time or venue to allow all family and friends to be present. As one might anticipate, the difference between fxC MES and outreach MES in their reporting of baptisms and confirmations is marked. It makes one wonder whether, when a Messy Church aims to be church, it starts to behave like it.

	All confirmations	Child confirmations
All MES	13%	9%
FxC MES	18%	11%
Outreach MES	7%	6%

Table 9. Confirmations in Messy Church

However, sometimes children are baptised as infants before they find their way to Messy Church, so that is not the whole picture. Yet in our attenders' research, around half of our modest-sized sample said their journey of following Jesus began with Messy Church.[33]

Of course, not all children are interested in what goes on at a Messy Church. We took advice that as part of adhering to good research ethics, we should provide an alternative activity for those children who did not want to take part. There were a few who joined in the creative exercise but didn't want to say anything in the interview. The children who did take part were unpredictable, enthusiastic and wonderfully straightforward in their responses. Children don't quite 'get' the need to answer research questions in the way that adults will, and it's very much a snapshot of what they are thinking in that moment.

Perhaps it was inevitable that if you talk about the *path* of following Jesus and give anyone a blank canvas to create something, they will paint something related to the natural world – a tree, a rainbow or an animal. In asking our children to choose made-up names to ensure confidentiality in disseminating findings, we had all sorts of references to creation. We offer that observation in *What Goes On Inside* as part of our findings. Is there something about childhood (and this particular childhood generation) raising awareness of our responsibility as caretakers of our environment – the fifth mark of mission in Anglicanism?[34]

79% of leaders in our sample of 174 reported that children no longer being an appropriate age was a key factor in people leaving Messy Churches.[35] Nevertheless, clearly some teenagers still attend. Aware of comments from critics that Messy Church cannot retain teenagers, more Messy Churches than we expected had some sort of follow-on provision, although sometimes the young people would have to seek it out at another place and time.[36]

What provision has Messy Church established for parents and children once children reach secondary school age?								
	Separate youth group	Teens serve as helpers	Further group/ activities	Changed MES to be youth focused	Confirmation	Intention only	Tried but no success	Other
All MES	28%	21%	8%	2%	1%	3%	2%	2%
FxC MES	33%	23%	8%	2%	2%	1%	2%	2%
Outreach MES	22%	20%	7%	1%	0%	5%	2%	1%

Table 10. Provisions for secondary-school-age children

At the risk of stating the obvious – knowing how important peers are at this stage of life and the lengths to which teenagers go to actively *avoid* spending time socially with their parents – it is no wonder that the family dynamic of attending a Messy Church together no longer works in the same way it did when children were younger.

We had fewer secondary school-aged children take part than under-11s – only a handful – and no older teenagers. Ours were extremely chatty and spoke very positively about Messy Church. With so few, it is impossible to know if their comments are typical of young people in this stage of life who attend. If you read *What Goes On Inside*, you must weigh their comments against your own experience of teenagers in Messy Church.

Varying adult journeys

The category of adult is deliberately broad, to include parent, grand-parent, carer, aunt, uncle, godparent, a family friend – possibly even an adult sibling. Here I am not including adult leaders, team members and volunteers, although our research flagged how much of a grey area it can be totally separating out adult attenders from adult team members. Some seasoned Christians on team told us they get just as much out of being involved as the children do and attend Messy Church as their primary place of church. Some adults very new to church life are invited on to the wider team as the next step in their discipleship.

Once again, this research was enriched by inclusion of the voices of attenders themselves, not only the leaders' interpretation of what they thought was going on for adult attenders. No doubt our method-ology helped create favourable conditions in requiring attenders to be interested enough in Messy Church to give up their time to take part. The modest number of those who did were very happy to participate and reflect on their own journey.

Anecdotally, in our telephone conversations with leaders of 174 Messy Churches, we heard of all sorts of challenges around adult attenders: adults assuming they can drop off their children and leave – much like a babysitting service – or one childminder bringing six children. We also heard of Messy Church enthusiasts who are highly mobile and will travel to different Messy Churches in the course of a month or even a week.

And then there is the tricky issue of adults bringing children to Messy Church and the vicar deems this as an indication of regular attendance at worship and signs the form for their children to apply for a church school. Like all existing churches, this issue is a hard one. You hope such adults have a positive enough experience that, though they may have come for dubious reasons, they stay for the right ones. And if they don't stay, how much is this a poor reflection of us or of them? Our adult confirmation statistics were modest but mildly encouraging. If parents are only coming for school admission, would they choose to be confirmed too? Within our sample of 174, the following percentage of Messy Churches reported at least one confirmation.[37] Once again, note the difference reported by fxC MES and outreach MES.

	All confirmations	Adult confirmations
All MES	13%	7%
FxC MES	18%	13%
Outreach MES	7%	2%

Table 11. Adult confirmation of Messy Church attenders

I imagine it would be extremely difficult for anyone within church circles to capture any concrete data on the prevalence of church attendance for the sake of obtaining admission to faith schools. Who would tell the truth to a church researcher? As a parent of a second-ary school-aged child myself – who wanted a good education for my child – I know this is a complex and highly emotive topic.

One of the smaller projects within the overall portfolio of the *Playfully Serious* research followed up some families who had attended Messy Church regularly for a while but had since left. Not only did it reveal some continued involvement in church life, but it also indicated the reasons adults brought their children in the first place. Adults most often reported that they brought their children to Messy Church to give them an introduction to Christian faith.[38]

It always strikes me as somewhat bizarre that adults might not be churchgoers (or even Christians) *themselves*, but still want their chil-dren to learn about the Christian faith and to experience something of church for themselves should they wish to stick with it when they're older. It feels a bit like your child learning a musical instrument if you don't play one. But like it or not, this is the surprising mission context we find ourselves in and – odd though it may seem – it is an oppor-tunity we shouldn't always assume we will have in years to come.

It has been interesting to encounter the first-hand cynicism around Messy Church as clergy have encountered this research. For example, some still equate Messy Church with Sunday school. Up to a point they may be right, as Messy Church is nothing new or novel; it works with craft and storytelling and food – things that the church has always done to some extent. But, as Bob Jackson writes in *Messy Church Theology*, whereas the Sunday school movement prioritised child education (the acquiring of knowledge), in Messy Church there is the potential to encourage conversations of faith between adults and children as part of whole-of-life discipleship.[39] This includes children talking about faith with adults who aren't their parents, as mentioned in *What Goes On Inside*.[40]

At a fairly crude level, we tried to measure this element of informal spiritual conversation.[41] Maybe the misunderstanding that Messy Church is only a fun thing for children is the inevitable conclusion some draw if the Messy Church they go to ticked the 'never' box about such conversations. But note how few respondents ticked this.

How often are there informal spiritual conversations at your Messy Church?					
	Never	Occasionally	Frequently	Very often	Don't know
All MES	5%	64%	21%	5%	5%
FxC MES	3%	60%	27%	5%	3%
Outreach MES	7%	67%	15%	5%	6%

Table 12. Spiritual conversations at Messy Church

Part of the cynicism around Messy Church might also be to do with a hesitation on the part of wider church life to embrace the creative arts. Music is inherent to church life, and you might find a bit of dancing, flag-waving or drama at certain types of churches. But, on the whole, other than banner-making or flower-arranging, it feels as though our churches sideline art somehow. Much has been written elsewhere on church and the arts as uncomfortable bedfellows. Artists 'sense the church is uneasy with the arts because the former cannot control the output of the latter… They argue the church at large is ignorant, of art, its discipleship and purpose.'[42]

Yet, some of the adult participants reported being greatly helped by the creative style of engagement in Messy Church. They felt 'more at home' here than in more traditional types of church.

> When you do Messy Church it's like totally different to the rest of the services and it just sort of gives that 'Yeah, I do need to grow… I've got a whole life to live.'
> Skye, adult

> The team are all really lovely… It's my calm place even when it's crazy. I feel safe.
> Sally, adult

> It's deepening learning… It's so much more practical… that very practical aspect of making mistakes and drawing comparisons with your own life through stories, maybe than I guess in comparison to a more structured service. There's not necessarily that time for exploration and application.
> Heidi, adult[43]

For those who are artistic – certainly those who are artistic by profession – there is a danger that they only bring part of themselves into church life, never their whole self. I am not wanting to say that starting or joining a Messy Church is the inevitable calling of anyone artistic. Rather, the interactive approach to exploring faith through art and craft was appreciated by some adults who felt that it deepened their learning and challenged them about the whole of their lives more so than other types of services. Seen in this light, developing spiritual retreat experiences for Messy Church adult attenders based around the arts (with some rebranding) does seem a logical conclusion.

Some hold that Messy Church is like the shallow end of the swimming pool in terms of spirituality and discipleship.[44] I can certainly appreciate the challenges around how much adults can really share about their personal lives within earshot of children if adult topics are discussed. However, this research reminded us that the lives of adult attenders are not shallow. To listen to them talk, issues such as grieving the death of a loved one and mental health all surfaced fairly swiftly, even in short interviews.

Perhaps the shallowness is created when leaders place too much emphasis on the practicalities of set-up and getting people through the door, without enough space given to listening to attenders and what is going on in their lives as you build relationships. Given how manic a Messy Church can be, I do sympathise. In our sample, the median size of a Messy Church congregation was 43 people,[45] which is a lot of people to talk to in two hours.

All aspects of our research pointed to how busy family life can be these days. Our attenders talked of monthly attendance as being fairly regular for them in all that they juggle. Attenders also spoke of the *quality* of gatherings being more important than the quantity, which led us to conclude: where meeting more frequently reduces the quality of what you can deliver, think again.[46]

Adult journeys in faith

The 31% of Messy Churches who reported at least one 'new believer' or more is one of those statistics that can lead to quite different reactions.[47]

	New believers
All MES	31%
FxC MES	46%
Outreach MES	16%

Table 13. Self-reproduction in Messy Church

Some might look at it and praise God for new people coming to faith in some of our Messy Churches. But others might ask, what does that say about the other 69% that didn't report new believers? Equally, what would many parishes honestly report? The 46% reported by the fxC MES should be celebrated; comparing this with the 16% of outreach MES, it is hard not to advocate for the fxC approach if one is committed to seeing new people come to faith.

Another very simple measure we attempted was gathering data on leaders' perception of changed lives.[48] Evidence that suggests a greater degree of life transformation in fxC MES is present in these percentages too.

How many people's lives have changed because of Messy Church?						
	None	A few	Some	Most	Don't know	No response
All MES	6%	42%	33%	6%	11%	1%
FxC MES	2%	39%	44%	9%	6%	0%
Outreach MES	11%	45%	22%	4%	17%	1%

Table 14. Lives changed through Messy Church

This kind of question has limitations: does a leader know a person well enough to make this kind of judgement? And is this measured in the big life changes or in the small, subtle things? As leaders, we know *our* journey of coming to faith hasn't always been a straightforward one. In terms of people coming along who know very little about the Christian faith and being very new to church language and culture, it was not at all surprising to hear leaders comment in the focus groups that adult attenders' faith 'waxes and wanes... none of our journeys are a trajectory... particularly when you're further back'.[49]

Clearly, there is further to go in taking adult attenders on a journey of faith. The challenge that Jesus did *not* offer the child is, of course, there for the adult attender. To follow Jesus requires fairly radical change.[50] One leader reflected at the end of a focus group interview:

'It just hadn't occurred to me, the question of what happened to parents – when their children moved on… However much Messy Church is for the family… but [it] hadn't really occurred to me.' If Messy Church is truly for the whole family – the adults as well – how can we pay better attention to what happens next for *adults* when their children stop going?

Questions to consider

1 How well are you listening to your children in Messy Church? Do you see glimpses of God at work in their lives?

2 If the all-age nature of Messy Church ever feels 'shallow', ask yourself what you learn from the youngest person in your life about what it is to be human. What do you learn from the oldest person about what it is to be human?

3 Are there adults at your Messy Church who find creative arts life-giving? How could the arts help them explore their spirituality more deeply in another setting?

4 Are there helpers on your team who could be designated chaplains or pastors?

5 Are there helpers on your team who have the gift of personal evangelism? Are they freed up from other responsibilities to exercise this gift?

3

A leadership team's journey

*Pointing the way – setting the pace –
removing obstacles from the path*

Working as a team

Obvious though it may be, it is important to state at this point that Messy Churches are generally led by more than one leader. This gave my quantitative research colleagues a headache as they wrestled to analyse an uneven and untidy leadership resource across our sample. We differentiated between those who shoulder the overall responsibility for a Messy Church and those who help 'on the day' with food, craft or set-up/clear-up. For the former, we use the term 'core team' and for the latter, 'wider team'.

This collaborative approach is an interesting conundrum; there are real and obvious strengths for volunteer leaders who are time-poor facilitating a gathering that requires practical preparation. In my experience, the larger the team leading, the more time (and energy) it takes to communicate and delegate. Anyone who has read *The Human Face of the Church*[51] knows that working with large teams of volunteers in church can be fraught with unforeseen difficulties. It is a huge accomplishment when such collaborative leadership happens smoothly month in, month out.

For the core team, my colleague Dave Lovell created a graphic to represent visually those who take overall leadership responsibility for making Messy Church happen. I hope you notice, as we did, the important leadership contribution we have from women, especially those who are lay people, those who volunteer and those who contribute in their spare time. On one level, we anticipated this leadership data to a degree, especially having gathered data on Messy Church from *The Day of Small Things*. Nonetheless, *Playfully Serious* has been an opportunity to name this reality and acknowledge this valuable leadership resource that sometimes goes unnoticed.

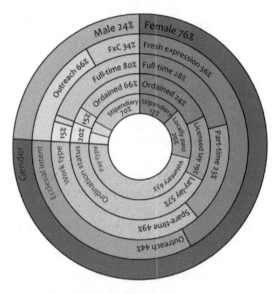

Diagram 1 Leadership in Messy Church

The indigenous leadership figures in teams reported in our sample were very encouraging, especially in the more deprived parts of the country where local church life can seem a bit thin in terms of the leadership resource. Even in the areas in the highest deprivation rankings, 36% of Messy Churches reported local people becoming part of the leadership team.

Being intentional about discipleship

Looking to the part of *Playfully Serious* that captured the perspectives of core team leaders, what did they say about discipleship? The *Managing the Mess* report offers the summarised material in full, organised thematically; it offers deeper, more detailed comment than the telephone calls to leaders allowed us. In focus group interviews, leaders noted the obvious tension in the fact that effective discipleship in Messy Church would be strengthened by main gatherings being more than monthly, but that it's already a 'hard juggling act'.[52]

Leaders identified external dynamics that they felt were largely beyond their control. Parents working long hours, families unexpectedly moving away and children alternating weekend visits when parents are divorced all contribute to difficulties in matching up Messy Church with the natural rhythm of attenders' lives. Unpredictable attendance makes it hard for both very low and very high attendance. When it's busy, one leader said, 'The team can feel "whoa it's all a bit busy there" and actually… I wouldn't be able to tell you who was there, because there's so many people that you just don't get to see and engage with everybody.'[53]

With a lot of attenders with non-churched backgrounds, leaders talked of linguistic and cultural barriers to be negotiated. Spiritual journeying is too deep and delicate a process to undertake hastily. Inclusivity and accessibility were cited as important, so to introduce the language of discipleship felt like unhelpful churchy terminology, but leaders didn't know of another term to use. In inviting parents to something outside Messy Church, one leader said, 'We don't quite know how we're gonna pitch it… worried I'm gonna scare people away.'[54]

When asked 'How do you recognise first steps in discipleship?', leaders talked of attenders asking questions, families supporting other families, loyalty in attending Messy Church gatherings and involvement in other aspects of wider church life. One leader reflected that the 'disciples walked along, [Jesus] walked with them, talking to them…

It was only at the very end when he said he was going to go that they recognised him for who he was… and that's what we're doing at Messy Church, we're on that walk to Emmaus.'[55] These 'walking alongside' instincts might be a factor in the high percentages fxC MES reported for one-to-one discipleship and inviting adults to serve on team. These percentages can be seen in the table below.

Many leaders struggled to envision *deeper* discipleship. As one leader said, 'I don't know what counts as deeper.'[56] Attention around watching for something deeper didn't seem to be as present – or at least not in a way that leaders could readily articulate to us. 'You might be very hopeful that they become disciples, but it's not in our heads,' one leader commented. And in the course of asking about discipling methods in our sample of 174, this table shows us that 17% of leaders admitted discipleship wasn't their intention, or 36% were expecting to see or were seeing discipleship happen for attenders through the wider parish.[57]

Discipling methods	All MES	FxC MES	Outreach MES
Discipleship through wider parish	36%	38%	35%
Adults serving in teams	32%	43%	21%
One-to-one	31%	47%	15%
Small groups	29%	36%	22%
Children/teens serving in teams	28%	33%	23%
Other	26%	40%	12%
Intention only	12%	9%	15%
Not our intention	17%	1%	33%

Table 15. Ways of discipling in Messy Churches

Some leaders suggested that 'shared concepts in language' were important; they were mindful that subjectivity and nuance may mean you think you've explained an aspect of discipleship clearly, but you can't always assume attenders have grasped the implications fully. A shared pool of simple narratives and personal stories seemed to be the most helpful with a group of mixed age and church experience. Berryman observes that children learn language more quickly than adults, so finding ways to explain and explore discipleship will directly benefit younger members even if adults struggle to keep up.[58]

The need for some degree of interaction linked into another theme that emerged. Two focus group participants were reflecting on the take-home resources that they give to families. One said, 'I've not ever had any feedback… whether it's used.' Another replied, 'We're the same… haven't even thought to ask for any feedback.'[59] As chapter 1 highlighted, there are varieties of ways that Messy Churches teach about worship and prayer, but it would help if leaders found out about how these are received by attenders.

Is running a Messy Church easy or hard?

On one level, running a Messy Church looks easy. If you're good at organising, chatting to parents at the school gate, designing crafts, laying on a meal, coordinating a team of volunteers – what's the problem? But in the focus groups with leaders, they named some of the more subtle demands that perhaps aren't as evident on the surface. As already discussed, they have the daunting task of engaging with a higher proportion of attenders with little knowledge about the Christian faith, and are expected to be able to nurture faith in both children and adults at the same time with no ministerial training, despite the well-known difficulties in leading good family services in existing church.[60]

Keeping the momentum up in the team can be difficult; some leaders are heroically managing most of it themselves. The ageing of many teams was cited as an issue and one that may become more common.[61] Some leaders have been going for years now – maybe more than a decade – and they are looking around for how they can find an exit strategy. Our survey work also threw into the mix a question about the leaders' perceptions of how confident their team were in sharing faith. While acknowledging that most teams are an uneven mix of those who are very confident with those who are very shy, these are the averages the leaders gave:

On a scale of 1–10, how natural to your team members is the sharing of their faith? (1 = unnatural, 10 = very natural)									
	1	2	3	4	5	6	7	8	9	10
All MES	1%	2%	8%	8%	22%	14%	16%	21%	3%	6%
FxC MES	0%	2%	9%	7%	17%	16%	15%	23%	3%	8%
Outreach MES	1%	2%	6%	9%	27%	13%	17%	19%	2%	4%

Table 16. Faith-sharing within the team

Have team members taken any training in faith-sharing?		
	Yes	No
All MES	29%	71%
FxC MES	34%	66%
Outreach MES	23%	77%

Table 17. Training in faith-sharing

Leaders in our focus groups were well aware of the cynicism, apathy and dismissiveness that outsiders sometimes have for Messy Church, at the same time as having to continue to advocate for it being more than a children's activity and more than just a bit of fun. While some say this way of doing mission with an off-the-shelf model isn't particularly edgy, leaders still have to live with the unknown and have to trust 'that whatever situation we're in with the people who have come through the door, you're trusting God for guiding you to provide what they need, and then trusting him to actually carry that work on.'[62]

Quite a few comments were made about the sense of leaders being stretched across too many roles within parish life. There is a burden of expectations placed upon them to fulfil other church duties on top of Messy Church, without apparent regard for the personal costs of labour in Messy ministry. 'People still expect you to clean... do the readings on Sunday, intercessions, etc... [when I haven't even] had the time to be able to go and visit all Messy families.'[63]

So what would it look like if we released a few leaders to *only* do Messy Church? Suppose we said they didn't have to be on the flower rota, organise the summer fair or type up the parish magazine each week, as well as all they do for Messy Church? I realise that may not be a popular suggestion in parishes with already stretched resources. Some commentators can be sceptical that Messy Church doesn't take people on a deeper journey of faith, but is that altogether fair if we're not releasing or enabling Messy Church leaders to have the time to have a go at doing this?

Leadership succession

Some leaders found being part of their Messy Church as life-giving; they wouldn't want to be anywhere else. Other comments suggested that people are willing to serve but they are at capacity and don't want to do too much more. As spare-time volunteer leaders, 'There's a lot and we're all quite busy... in a sense it's quite draining on the leadership [and] team... not to say it isn't rewarding as well, [but] I don't really want to do too much more.'[64]

When we asked 'Where (or in what ways) are Messy Churches vulnerable?', leadership stability or succession was most often cited. One leader told us that others in her church were willing to support their Messy Church, but added, 'If I said, "we're not going to do it any more", they'd say "oh, that's sad". But it wouldn't, I suspect, be picked up.'[65] Another employed by a church said, 'If I was made redundant or the church didn't have enough money to pay me... I don't think anybody else would necessarily take it on.'[66] This reminds me of the question we raised in *The Day of Small Things*: who looks after lay-led initiatives after the founder moves on?[67]

When enthusiastic lay leaders step down and the Messy Church stops because there is no one else to lead, I find myself thinking about the wisdom of church planting. For some, the linguistic move away from 'church plant' as a noun towards 'fresh expression of church' with all its variations has meant the wisdom of church (and congregation) planting as a verb has sometimes got lost or obscured along the way.

Church-planting wisdom would encourage current leaders themselves to plan for succession, taking responsibility for praying and planning who will take over – and the leaders mentoring the person or those persons into that role. Unlike our historic parish churches and our vacancy procedures, planted congregations like Messy Churches are not well-enough established or sophisticated enough to cope with gaps between leaders. They have no formal procedures to fall back on, and what is more they need leaders who will reproduce the values in other leaders and allow for relational continuity when connections with new families still feel fragile.

The support of a permission-giver

To use a term like 'permission-giver' makes it sound as though this role is fulfilled by one individual. In some cases, this is true, but in others, it is a number of people. In an Anglican setting, it could be a combination of the vicar, the rural or area dean (if clergy are spread thinly in your area), church wardens, the PCC treasurer or maybe a diocesan member of staff who supports you because what you're doing is either missional or working with children. Of the leaders in our sample, 34% were clergy themselves; do they need permission-givers too? Supportive PCCs? The encouragement of a bishop or archdeacon through a ministerial review?

If you are a potential permission-giver, please value the leadership gifts of your Messy Church leaders. Help them grow in their leadership skills. It may not need as much time and energy as it sounds. Sometimes it's just the odd hour or two of listening we can offer to someone to help them mull over a tricky mission or ministry issue that might get lost in the busyness of life otherwise.

Perhaps this is the point to say that there are some people in church life who will never get Messy Church – perhaps people are too 'old school', too uncomfortable around arts and crafts or too adult-focused to explore childhood spirituality. Or perhaps they are just not in that phase of young family life or it's hard to imagine themselves back into it. If you are a permission-giver in that category, make sure you don't just quietly withdraw and leave leaders unsupported because it's not your 'thing'.

These leaders need support to flourish, especially if they are trying to develop discipleship – just as a training incumbent would support a curate in learning how to lead a church in which discipleship is nurtured. For example, can permission-givers set an example in finding ways to explain and explore discipleship when the word itself is problematic?

The interpretation of absent permission-giving clergy at Messy Church was discussed in our focus groups. Some leaders saw clergy not being present as a lack of support. One leader said, 'Our previous vicar was very keen for me to start it, but actually never wanted to come… no interest, really.'[68] One focus group talked about the positive dynamic a clergy person has in some mission contexts when new families see 'someone with a dog-collar there… perhaps they might not [otherwise] see it as a valid part of the church'.[69]

In doing the research for *Playfully Serious* we were not asked to capture data from permission-giving clergy, so it is impossible to give their perspective. I have a working hypothesis that their absence does not necessarily mean lack of interest or support; I wonder if sometimes the reverse is true – their absence means they trust Messy Church leaders to lead, and they don't want to get in the way or cramp their style. Or possibly they are simply too busy. In some dioceses, numbers of stipendiary clergy are being dramatically reduced. Seeing fewer dog-collars might be something Messy Churches have no choice but to get used to.

Ironically, despite Messy leadership often being a collaborative endeavour, we were struck by the overall sense conveyed to us through these focus groups that it can still be a bit lonely. It reminded us a bit of the poem 'So I Stand by the Door' by Revd Samuel Shoemaker Jr, in which he reflects on church and mission.[70] The poem goes on to say that sometimes people inside the church don't really understand or appreciate those who are standing by the metaphorical door. It can feel lonely.

Questions to consider

1 Is there appropriate local recognition of the volunteer leaders who make Messy Church happen? Are they thanked on a regular basis?

2 Is the ministry of voluntary lay women in your congregation celebrated?

3 What level of spiritual retreat or leadership coaching would you like? Just because you may lead in a lay or voluntary capacity, this doesn't mean you can't seek out this kind of help. Who can you go to for exploring this further?

4 Have you and your team thought about leadership succession? Who might you mentor as potentially new leaders for when you step down? How might you best help them learn what to do and support them in their learning?

4

A Messy Church's journey

*Discerning the destination – carrying the bags –
keeping the group together*

As outlined in chapter 1, *Playfully Serious* was one of the first projects from Church Army's Research Unit after we widened the breadth of initiatives on which we were collecting data. For *The Day of Small Things*, having to exclude initiatives was justifiable for research purposes but regrettable from the perspective of encouraging a variety of mission endeavours.

Therefore, it was a delight to include outreach initiatives in this research and to be able to draw comparisons and make contrasts – especially across the statistical data in *Painting with Numbers*. Most tables and graphs so far in these chapters have faithfully reported separate findings as well as overall findings for you to make your own observations. This chapter will draw together a few further findings on discipleship depending on whether or not a Messy Church intends to be a fresh expression of church.

Is this really a different path or actually a similar one?

It can be subtle – more of an art than a science – in deciding which side of the definition a Messy Church falls. Within the ten definitional indicators,[71] by far the easiest criterion to weigh up is frequency. *The Day of Small Things* argued that it was too much of a stretch to believe that an initiative meeting less frequently than monthly would function as a *regular* worshipping congregation or be able to build community for those who attend.

Then, under the 'Is it missional?' criterion, it is relatively straight-forward to work out if a Messy Church is reaching new people. If you don't recognise families who come and haven't seen them at any other church services, then most of the time that would indicate new people. However, whether they have just snuck into Messy Church while also regularly attending a church across town is worth watching out for; it never hurts to raise this question casually in conversation just in case.

The criteria that are more difficult to weigh up (numbers 5 and 8) are to do with whether families in the longer term will continue to come only to Messy Church or whether they will find their way to existing congregational life on a Sunday morning. Leaders said there was sometimes a mix – some families making it to Sunday and some not. Working with this untidy reality, we settled this issue on whether the majority of families were not finding their way to Sunday morning (and looked like they may never) as the decider as to whether a Messy Church was aiming to be church for its attenders.

As the first three chapters of this section have highlighted, there are some common issues that any Messy Church faces, whether out-reach or fxC. How do we continue to see new families coming in, and how much should we chase when they seem to have drifted away? As a team, how do you become friends with these families, recog-nising needs and saying, 'I wanna walk a bit of this journey with you if I can.'[72] The Messy Church values are common across both types – how you live out being creative, hospitable, all-age, celebratory and Christ-centred.

Some might ask: if there is so much in common, why does it mat-ter whether a Messy Church is deemed fxC or outreach? The most important reason these categories matter is to do with who takes primary responsibility for the discipleship of families that attend. If a Messy Church is outreach – a stepping stone to belonging to other aspects of church life – then discipleship is a wider issue across the parish; Messy Church is just the way in.

But if a Messy Church intends to be a fresh expression of church – sometimes by choice, but sometimes a reluctant necessity if families don't start attending Sunday also – it falls on the shoulders of the Messy leadership to take responsibility for discipleship. For if this is church for these families, they will not get such things anywhere else. All the issues are intensified; if these dynamics are not working in the Messy Church, there is no wider parish or Sunday safety net to fall back on.

A journey of outreach

Of our sample of 174, 86 Messy Churches that said they intended to be outreach initiatives were inviting families to also come on a Sunday. In the course of our telephone calls, we double-checked that current intention matched their previous intention (at the point we had been in touch with them for *The Day of Small Things*) and only a small number had since decided they were called to a fresh expressions of church journey.

While BRF (The Bible Reading Fellowship, the home of Messy Church) literature generally advocates for Messy Churches to always think of themselves as church for the families that go, there are some contexts where developing as a fxC doesn't seem right. In traditional rural villages in which Christendom seems alive and well still, some families in the local community can't really get their heads around having more than one church congregation. To set up a complementary Messy Church congregation on another day of the week in a 1960s hall (rather than the beautiful Norman church) doesn't make sense to them.

Some larger churches that already have an internal network of smaller mission communities, outreach groups and mission activities for different age groups can find it hard to think of their Messy Church as its own congregation. It would beg the question: is the young people's ministry also its own congregation? And what does that make the women's fellowship or the mums-and-toddlers' ministry? Also, I think it can be hard to maintain ecclesial intentions if there is ecumenical partnership. For example, if an Anglican church (providing most of the team) and its Salvation Army neighbour (providing the venue) run a Messy Church together, if this were its own congregation, which denomination would 'own' it?

Based on our sample, we note with interest that 44% of outreach MES met on Saturdays,[73] which was not a feature of fxC MES, who preferred weekdays or Sunday. Male, ordained, full-time stipendiary leaders were more likely (66%) to lead an outreach MES, which is an intriguing finding. Does it suggest that this type of leader works instinctively with a more attractional approach than other types of leaders?

As the statistics in the previous chapters have illustrated, there are drawbacks to outreach MES if one is serious about discipleship of attenders within Messy Church itself. As previously noted, more modest percentages of attempting discipleship through one-to-one engagement or inviting newcomers to join the team were reported in outreach MES.[74] The baptism and Communion statistics suggested less progress compared with fxC MES, and the reports of any aspect of life transformation were markedly lower.

Turning to the practical issue of finance, the use of collections or donations was less common in outreach MES, but there were no significant differences between churches at different levels of deprivation or geographical context. Perhaps this is not surprising if a parish allocates mission budget to initiatives understood to be outreach. As such, outreach MES were more likely (67%) to be dependent on their sending churches.

	Collections/ donations	Covering running costs	Regular givers	None	Grants/ fundraising	Other	Intention only
All MES	73%	30%	28%	13%	11%	8%	3%
FxC MES	82%	35%	32%	6%	10%	9%	2%
Outreach MES	64%	26%	24%	20%	13%	6%	5%

Table 18. How funds are raised in Messy Church

When we engaged in some modest follow-up on why Messy Church types closed or died, there was no significant difference between the types. Outreach MES were just as likely to cease as fxC MES. What was different were the reasons cited; outreach MES identified mission reasons – numbers dwindling – whereas for fxC MES, reasons were to do with the departure of the leader.[75]

A journey of a fresh expression of church

Of our sample of 174, 88 Messy Churches said that they intended to be fresh expressions of church, with a few changing to a journey of outreach. I must commend Messy Church as a movement where many of its leaders understand and are quick to advocate more widely that Messy Churches should be seen as church. Yet, I want to offer an observation here: I hear some leaders say, 'It is church for them', but go on to explain that this is because Messy Church is the only thing families come to. This is not quite the same as saying, 'It is church for them because we are planting a new congregation.'

Furthermore, it's no wonder we're all a bit stumped when we come to think about ecclesial maturity. We know it's about discipleship, but what else? Equally, ecclesial vulnerability is a bit of a mystery. And for the pragmatists among us, until someone has explained why such questions are directly relevant to everyday life, they are easy to ignore.

Perhaps it is no wonder then that outreach and fxC MES end up looking very similar to the casual observer.

I suspect we – and by that I mean researchers and fresh expressions of church commentators – are probably to blame for this lack of understanding, because it is us who talk easily about ecclesial maturity and vulnerability as if they are terms used regularly in the course of daily church life. Of course, they are not. These terms are part of the vocabulary used by planters of churches and it is this planting instinct that is at the heart of the fresh expressions of church intention.

As already touched on, what is the wisdom we've learnt in the last 40 years of church planting that could also apply to fxC MES? Besides the very necessary work around developing discipleship, what else can one focus on? In an Anglican context, sacraments are an obvious area to develop. Out of our sample of 174, 107 hadn't yet engaged with sacraments, so there is still plenty of scope for development. *Painting with Numbers* details which sacraments – baptism, confirmation and communion – had been engaged with, and reports higher engagement by fxC MES compared with outreach MES.[76]

I know celebrating both baptism and Communion can be fraught with difficulty. If a family have requested a baptism in Messy Church, do you hold it in your usual after-school meeting time or have a bespoke Messy Church gathering at another time? Who does the baptism preparation? When do you introduce teaching around Communion? Is your permission-giver supportive? In our focus groups, one leader shared their experience that once one Messy Church baptism had happened, more requests followed – almost as if people have to experience a 'Messy baptism' first-hand to understand the possibilities.

Within the community dimension, how do you help fxC MES develop more of a sense of oneness – that attendance isn't just whoever turns up, but developing friendships across families? Some of the literature invites Messy Churches to consider meeting weekly as a response to this. In some ways it would be lovely; still, a touch of realism is needed as to what will be sustainable in the longer term. 67% of our sample met monthly and some of the attenders described monthly as 'frequent' for them and their families.

In the busyness of life, it can be hard to get families to come to extra things. But that doesn't mean there can't be connection between gatherings. Some examples that surfaced in this research included: prayer request email groups, social media chat groups, meal rotas for families in tough times, babysitting, social outings or Christian conferences.

Another area of potential maturity is the relationship a Messy Church has with its wider parish. *The Day of Small Things* showed us that Messy Church has a close, symbiotic relationship with inherited church; currently I know of only one Anglican Messy Church that has been planted as its own church with legal and financial independence. Across our sample of 174, we asked a simple question about the relationship they had with their sending church.[77]

	Very dependent on sending church	Partially dependent on sending church	Becoming able to exist in our own right	Working at the inter-dependence of giving and receiving
All MES	47%	32%	10%	12%
FxC MES	26%	38%	19%	17%
Outreach MES	67%	26%	1%	6%

Table 19. Being catholic – degrees of maturity and dependency on the sending church in Messy Churches

Knowing how to be a church within a church sounds a bit odd at first, but, in an Anglican context, that is the reality at national, diocesan, deanery and parish level. This is one way we express our catholicity. How can we apply the ways we are part of the wider church, yet also distinct to congregations, within parish life?

One of the ways is having representation on the decision-making councils of the church. As I write this, I'm wincing at the thought of compelling time-poor Messy leaders to go to any more meetings than they do already. However, there is an important issue: does your Messy Church have enough formal representation on the PCC to lend it some stability, recognition and clout? When asked, our 174 leaders reported the following:

	Leadership team	Informal PCC rep.	Formal PCC rep.	None	Intention only	Other
All MES	76%	51%	14%	7%	3%	2%
FxC MES	85%	52%	19%	1%	2%	5%
Outreach MES	67%	49%	8%	13%	5%	0%

Table 20. Self-governing in Messy Churches

Here are some further questions to test whether your Messy Church is perceived as a fresh expression of church:

- Is your Messy Church part of your annual general meeting reporting?
- When your parish is in vacancy, is it part of the parish profile?
- Does the parish website list Messy Church under its 'Worshipping congregations' drop-down menu or its 'Activities' or 'Events' drop-down menu?
- When the volunteer numbers seem to shrink, is it more likely there is a rushed notice given on a Sunday morning for a few extra pairs of hands instead of the person leading the intercessions praying that God would draw to this Messy Church congregation the right leaders?

These are all small but subtle ways to communicate a Messy Church is its own worshipping congregation, and they offer some protection if and when leaders step down. Applying church-planting wisdom to parish life remains a big mindset shift. If you add to this the real-ity that 'there is a finite number of resources [within] an established

church',[78] it is even more difficult to imagine planting something new
and further. The final pages of the *Playfully Serious* summary booklet
recommend that leaders that it will always be a struggle for some to
see their Messy Church as a congregation. Make sure the right people
understand what you are trying to do and then let your ministry speak
for itself.

A fresh expression of church journey does ask a lot of its volunteer
leaders. I remember one phone call with a leader who expressed an
overwhelming sense of guilt that the Messy Church she led as a fxC
hadn't achieved more, sooner. She had realised the full implications
of what being church meant. She wondered if some Messy Churches
needed to be released from the burden of expectation to be a congregation and the sense of continually underperforming. Nevertheless,
research findings do show a fxC approach does develop discipleship
further than outreach MES.

I finish my contribution to this book with a comment on the self-
reproducing dynamics of Messy Church. 19% of all Messy Churches
reported further outreach activities and, as already noted, 34%
reported indigenous leaders.

	Indigenous leaders	New believers	More virtuous lives	Further outreach	Further fxC	Others inspired from a visit to you	New ordinands
All MES	34%	31%	31%	19%	3%	40%	3%
FxC MES	43%	46%	46%	22%	5%	57%	3%
Outreach MES	24%	16%	15%	16%	1%	23%	2%

Table 21. Self-reproducing in Messy Church

Given that in many cases Messy Churches have started with nothing –
no budget, no full-time paid leader, no dedicated building for their
exclusive use, main gathering often meeting no more than monthly –
I am amazed at the sense that many are building something from

nothing and seeing ongoing momentum. I look forward to seeing how the journey of the overall movement continues to unfold.

Questions to consider

1   Which journey do you sense your Messy Church is called to? More of just the outreach dynamic or a journey of becoming church together?

2   What emotions do you carry as leaders – especially those who are effectively congregation planters/leaders? Surprise? Frustration? Fulfilment? Exhaustion? Do you talk about these emotions as a team or with your permission-giver and find the space to process them?

3   What one thing could your Messy Church focus on in the coming year? What would help it evolve in a healthy way? Pray for those areas you want to develop.

Part II

Discipleship through the lens of the Messy Church values

Christ-centred   All-age   Creativity   Hospitality   Celebration

5

Christ-centred

Tom Donoghue

Tom Donoghue is the evangelist at Cliff College, helping to equip the church for evangelism and mission. He leads the Cliff Year (gap year) and is a member of the Methodist Church Evangelism and Growth Team, where his work is focused on young evangelists. He loves Messy Church and is a member of the national support teams.

Messy Church is Jesus' church. A cheerful welcome and sitting around tables to enjoy a good meal together makes God's generosity known through our hospitality; in the thoughtful planning and the range of activities, it reveals the creativity of God; there is a celebration of God throughout, but it is particularly noticeable as everybody sings (with actions) to praise him; and it is open to all ages worshipping Christ together. Underpinning those four values – hospitality, creativity, celebration and all-age – is one other Messy value, Christ-centred. It is this value which turns all that happens at Messy Church - from being well fed, to having wonderful conversations across generations, to seeing a Bible story dramatised - into a Spirit-filled experience.

Jesus shared stories with all kinds of people – women and men, adults and children, rich and poor, the sick and the healthy, the social outcasts and the elite, people who were like him and people who were not. He had a story to share and was consistent in his message of love and hope for all people from God.

At the end of Matthew's gospel, Jesus commissions his disciples (including us):

> All authority in heaven and on earth has been given to me. Therefore go and make disciples of all nations, baptising them in the name of the Father and of the Son and of the Holy Spirit, and teaching them to obey everything I have commanded you. And surely I am with you always, to the very end of the age.
> MATTHEW 28:18–20

Jesus tells us that he wants to be at the centre of our lives and he wants to be at the centre of the lives of the people that we meet, know and love. He asks us to join in with telling his story; this can fill us with dread and worry, and even fear, as we wonder: what if I get it wrong? What if they have questions that I can't answer? What happens if they don't like what I say and never come back? But Jesus, the great storyteller, promises that he is with us always and gives us a great confidence that we are filled with Christ's Spirit. He will guide us and empower us when we speak and share his story of love and hope.

Let us take a moment to reflect on our own journey to faith in Jesus Christ. What did it look like for you when you were investigating the Christian faith? Do you know how old you were when you became a Christian? Is there a significant moment that you can look back on and pinpoint or did your faith develop gradually over time? And who else was a part of your journey? Did a parent believe and share stories with you? Did a teacher at school or church or a youth worker help you to explore the Bible stories? Did a friend talk to you about their own Christian faith?

For many of us, our path of discipleship began before we identified ourselves as a member of the Christian faith. For most of us, our discipleship journey is an experience of which other people are a significant part. Research carried out in 2015–16, called *Talking Jesus*,[79] shows that for an adult practising Christian, the second most influential factor in becoming a Christian was having conversations with a Christian. This factored more highly for them than attending a standard church service, reading the Bible, having an experience of the love of Jesus and an unexplained spiritual experience, and was only less influential than growing up in a Christian family. Jesus has commissioned us to make disciples, to teach them his commandments, and he has promised that he will be always be with us, to guide us as we speak and share his story of love and hope.

When our Messy Church incorporates the value of being Christ-centred, it not only means that Jesus is at the centre, but it also means that Messy Church is church! It is a place for the team, the regular and the first-time visitor to meet Christ and to experience a foretaste of heavenly community as we gather together, at different stages of our faith journey, willing to share in that journey with one another.

The wonderful thing about Messy Church is that we can share Christ's story across the generations, and we know that our efforts are not just for our friends but will continue to give God the glory into the next generation and beyond. As Christ-centred people, we are willing to trust Christ's long-term perspective:

I will tell you a story. I will tell you about things from the past that are hard to understand. We have heard the story, and we know it well. Our fathers told it to us. And we will not forget it. Our people will be telling this story to the last generation. We will all praise the Lord and tell about the amazing things he did… So they would all trust in God, never forgetting what he had done and always obeying his commands.

PSALM 78:2–4, 7 (ERV)

One of the challenges in Messy Church is making sure that it is Christ-centred. Our time together is busy and fun, and sometimes we can forget why we are really there. It can easily turn into an event, because we are so busy cutting out crafts and playing games that we forget to have a conversation about the Bible story; we imagine there will be a chance to share in conversation over dinner, but then get caught up with serving the food and helping with the washing-up.

In 2016 I started a Messy Church with the support of my church, and it took us all by surprise when it launched and a large number of people attended (including the team of volunteers and all the adults and children who attended, there were over 90 people at our first Messy Church). We had no idea how many people to expect, and had thought we had been over-generous in catering for no more than 50 people. We had to run to the local supermarket to buy more food! It was a great joy to start in this way, but it also meant that we needed to put steps in place to make sure that it didn't turn into an event that we just added to the list of church programmes. It needed to be more about the relationships with the people who joined us and less about the numbers who signed in at the welcome desk. While we recognised that we needed to continue to have a spectacular range of activities on offer for all ages, we also needed to make sure there was an opportunity for fruitful conversations to be had.

I decided to gather as many of the team as possible a couple of weeks before each month's Messy Church. This was not a time to prepare and plan but an opportunity to disciple one another and equip ourselves spiritually for the upcoming Messy Church. We met on a Saturday morning so that it didn't disrupt the weekend too much, and we called it 'Messy Breakfast' and made sure it included all of the Messy values.

At Messy Breakfast, I would welcome everyone with breakfast laid out on the table, and we would enjoy a creative activity together, based on the Bible passage of the next Messy Church session. We would share a short Bible study, and we did this in a variety of ways to keep us fresh and to remind ourselves that for many people coming to Messy Church it is a new experience. We also made sure that it was open to all involved with Messy Church. It mainly attracted the team, but it was also a great place to grow deeper in our relationships with new volunteers who were starting to help at Messy Church since attending with their families. It also gave us quality time to share stories from the last session. We would all be so tired once Messy Church finished that everyone understandably just wanted to go home. It also gave us time to pray for the people coming to Messy Church, a meaningful and purposeful time of prayer together. It was a reminder of why we do Messy Church and helped us to keep Christ at the centre.

Our Messy Breakfast discipleship time began to see an impact on the discipleship in the wider Messy Church. We benefitted from an overflow of love, prayer and spending time 'being' with one another and God, instead of 'doing' with one another. The people who had come to the Messy Breakfast were more familiar with the Bible story; we had discussed it together and had two weeks to read it again on our own. It gave us time to really work out what the activity we were leading meant in the context of the story and opened us up to more natural and authentic conversations which linked into the Bible story. The team's confidence grew as we were able to support one another spiritually and relationally. We had already committed to praying together before each Messy Church started, and I noticed that since the introduction of the Messy Breakfasts the team prayed with more confidence and became more Christ-centred.

When Jesus prays in John 17, he prays not only for the disciples but also for those who will believe in him through their message. He prays that all of them will be one. Jesus prays that we will experience with one another a relationship like Jesus has with the Father; that we will be close and intimate with one another; that we will be of one heart and one mind; that not only will Jesus be in each of us, but we will be unified together. Jesus says that this will be attractive to those who don't yet know him and will draw them in and will make known to them the love of God.

As an evangelist, I think this is a point to reflect on: for our Messy Churches to be disciple-making churches, we need to be a team. Messy Church requires all sorts of people in all sorts of roles to help make it a success, and we need to be unified in our purpose. The communities we live in need more than a great monthly event; they need to see a unified group of people who love and care for one another and them. This means we need to put relationships first – we need to take time to be with one another as a team – so that we don't treat Messy Church as a task to be accomplished each month but rather as a journey to share.

As we become more relational as a team, we will see ourselves become more relational with the people who are coming to Messy Church. We will show them what it is like to be a Christ-centred person. As followers of Jesus, we need to always be Christ-centred, so as we go about our day we are either introducing people to who Jesus is or enriching their Christian faith.

Discipleship must include being in loving relationship with our siblings in Christ, and this is not only the goal but also a way of life. In Paul's first letter to the Corinthians, he explains that the Spirit unites us as one body: 'Now you are the body of Christ, and each one of you is a part of it' (1 Corinthians 12:27). This image helps us to understand how all the different parts of the body serve one another and reminds us that, although we may be diverse, we are united as one.

As a body, our Messy Church benefits from a range of talents as we all come to it with our own gifts, skills and personality. We benefit from being a variety of people and are able to trust that we have all been placed there by God. The environment and ambience allow all parts of the body to play to their strength, and it benefits those who are yet to make Christ the centre of their life. The Messy Church format means the congregation is able to spend time with many parts of the body as they move from the welcome at the door to the activities in the room, to the celebration of the story and praising God, to sitting down to a meal as they interact with the whole team.

The Messy Church format has taught us that discipling cannot be the responsibility of one person, because nobody has all the gifts that are needed to enable us to grow to the full maturity of Christ. A mature disciple will have a deep care for the others who are a part of the Messy Church, because they understand that this is a journey which we travel together. We share in the suffering of our friends as well as being able to rejoice with them when they flourish. If our Messy Church is like a family, it is providing a nurturing environment in which we can all experience the love and teaching which comes through our Messy Church values.

It takes a whole Messy Church to raise disciples. As the team disciples one another, the overflow will bring this relationship to everyone who comes through the doors. The long-term relationships that can be made among the whole team will be more transformative than they would be if they were dependent on one leader to engage and disciple a whole congregation. We need to take the people more seriously than the programmes that we are running. Being Christ-centred stops us being functional and creating a system in which we process people through. Instead, we are offered an opportunity to make friends and invest in long-term relationships, which, to the local community, looks different and is attractive. It is in this space that our families will be able to encounter Christ and not just hear about him, as they experience Jesus' love and character through us.

Jesus had a team around him. His disciples and followers can be categorised into different levels of relationship with him. First, there was the multitude that followed him and came to listen to his teaching. The crowds were so big that he went up on a mountainside or into a boat in order to be able to speak to them all. Then there were the 72, who must have benefitted from further teaching and had been able to learn about ministry from Jesus, as he sent them out to tell those they met that the kingdom of God was near to them (Luke 10:1–12). A closer group was the twelve disciples, who benefitted from deeper teaching with Jesus about the kingdom of God. Jesus held an even closer relationship with three of them, Peter, James and John, who had experienced a more intimate teaching and were there at some very personal times in Jesus' ministry and life, such as the transfiguration (Matthew 17:1–8) and when he called out to God in prayer the night before he died (Matthew 26:37–38).

No leader is able to disciple every single person who comes to Messy Church – you are unlikely to have the time to invest in each person. You will run out of energy, and you alone do not have all the spiritual gifts. Jesus recognised his own human limitations and invested in the three, then the twelve, then the 72 and then the multitude, equipping each of these groups so that they felt able and confident to take a lead in the ministry and discipleship.

I think of Peter fixing his eyes on Jesus when he fulfils Jesus' command to get out of the boat and walk on water. It is when we are stretched to do what seems impossible that we often see growth. The great commission's call to make disciples may feel like an impossible mission, but when we make discipleship central to our team, it begins to make the call a lot easier, as we can support one another and build each other up. It becomes our culture and a natural way to include everyone at Messy Church. As Messy followers of Pioneer Jesus, we are following in his footsteps, like many have done before us. We have an opportunity to bring the good news to new people, knowing that we follow in the trailblazer's footsteps:

Do you see what this means – all these pioneers who blazed the way, all these veterans cheering us on? It means we'd better get on with it. Strip down, start running – and never quit!… Keep your eyes on *Jesus*, who both began and finished this race we're in. Study how he did it. Because he never lost sight of where he was headed – that exhilarating finish in and with God – he could put up with anything along the way: Cross, shame, whatever. And now he's *there*, in the place of honour, right alongside God. When you find yourselves flagging in your faith, go over that story again, item by item, that long litany of hostility he ploughed through. *That* will shoot adrenaline into your souls!

HEBREWS 12:1–3 (MSG)

As we engage in Jesus' calling on us to lead, help and serve at our Messy Church; as we deal with the exhausting challenge that this ministry can be; as we work with limited resources when there seems to be so much to do; as we battle the tendency to try to maintain control – let us personally fix our eyes on Jesus. This will alter our perspective and ensure that our Messy Church is centred on our Christ.

6

All-age

Chris Barnett

Chris Barnett is based at the Centre for Theology and Ministry (Melbourne, Australia) in a role that encompasses responsibility for intergenerational ministry (children and their families) across the Uniting Church Synod of Victoria and Tasmania. This role includes a strong emphasis on intergenerational engagement, with a focus on consultancy, advocacy, resourcing and training. Chris is a keen participator and resourcer across a variety of networks, including the Australian Intergenerational Roundtable and the Australian Messy Church Roundtable.

Have you ever considered an elevator speech for Messy Church? How might one summarise the heart of the gloriously diverse adventure that is Messy Church in just 30 seconds? If the opportunity serendipitously arose to give a key leader of a congregation, faith community or denomination a snapshot of the essence of Messy Church, what might someone say? Some might comment on the colour, the creativity and the craft. Some might major on the mess, the meal and the making of friends. There's so much that could be said to inspire and encourage engagement with Messy Church. For me, though, my elevator speech focuses on three key words – 'all-age', 'discipleship' and 'community'.

What excites and energises me most about Messy Church is the vision for creating new communities of people of all ages growing in their following of Jesus together – young and old, the not-so-young and not-so-old, gathering together to experience, to explore and to express the great love of God as revealed in Christ; people of all ages, all abilities, all faith stories (from none whatsoever to the fully committed) having the opportunity to discover, deepen and delight in their engagement with God, God's world and their place in God's world. Framed in the language of discipleship, my passion for Messy Church is to see more disciples (of all ages) and more communities living out discipleship in response to God's gracious invitation to abundant life. What might your Messy Church elevator speech be?

'All-age', 'discipleship' and 'community' – to unpack these ideas in the context of Messy Church will take much longer than 30 seconds. Indeed, even this chapter will not be enough! However, as a starting point, I invite you to briefly consider Messy Church as all-age discipleship *community*. First and foremost, this places a focus on the priority of the relational dimension of Messy Church. Messy Church is not a programme; it is a community of people – sometimes gathered together, more often apart – connected to one another through relationships and shared experiences. Messy Church is not an event to attend but a community to belong to – and contribute to. Messy Church is not just about receiving or just about giving; it is a community where participants of all ages have the opportunity to both give and receive. Messy Church is not a place that privileges age; it is instead a community where all ages are valued equally, given opportunity to be engaged meaningfully and respectfully honoured as made in the image of God.

Messy Church is not just a community for all ages; it is rather a *discipleship* community *of* all ages. Messy Church is a place of and for discipleship, both individual and collective. Messy Church is a community comprising a range of disciples and discipleship experiences (from those who have no prior experience of what it means to be a follower of Jesus to those whose experience has been lifelong). A potentially helpful image for Messy Church (as opposed to the unhelpful image of stepping stones) is that of a pathway. In fact, a *discipleship* pathway where all ages can journey together – a pathway of exploring and learning; a pathway on which faith can be discovered, tried on, owned and lived out; a pathway that begins with God and continues with God along the way. Messy Church as an 'all-age discipleship community'? How exciting, and what a privilege to belong to such a church!

So far, so good. However, have you ever wondered what makes Messy Church *really* Messy Church? 'All-age', 'discipleship' and 'community' are not elements unique to Messy Church. When an existing inherited church embraces Messy Church, what is it actually embracing? When an existing church community signs up as a Messy Church, what are they signing up to? At the centre of Messy Church sit the five core values: being all-age, celebration, being Christ-centred, creativity and hospitality. In regular Messy Church gatherings these values are lived out through the three phases of Messy activities, Messy celebration (worship) and a Messy meal. In any other expressions of the Messy Church community that take place between the regular gatherings, these core values are similarly to be expressed. Arguably, what makes Messy Church *really* Messy Church is the unique combination of these values lived out intentionally within the context of an all-age discipleship *community*.

Turning our attention to discipleship, we can similarly wonder as to what discipleship *really* is. The Church Army *Discipleship Definitions*[80] paper helpfully canvasses a range of perspectives. The title itself, in the plural, points to the diversity of views on the matter. A variety of academics, authors, leaders, ministers, missiologists, practitioners and theologians articulate different understandings. A survey of different denominations, let alone specific congregations and individuals within such denominations, and theological traditions would yield similarly varied outcomes. While not wanting to claim an overarching 'Messy Church' understanding of discipleship, nevertheless some views may resonate more strongly in particular Messy Church communities – with many Messy Churches, for example, being significantly shaped by the writing of Paul Moore in *Making Disciples in Messy Church*[81] and Andrew Roberts in *Holy Habits*.[82] By way of a working definition, for the purposes of this chapter, Christian discipleship is an intentional following and learning from Jesus that is accompanied by specific actions that embody and encourage living in Jesus' way.

If Messy Church is an all-age discipleship community in which the values of all age, celebration, Christ-centred, creativity and hospitality are lived out; if Christian discipleship involves intentional, Jesus-centred living, learning and doing – what's next in our consideration of Messy Church and discipleship through the all-age lens? I suggest that the important question to address is, 'What kind of environment is most likely to sustain lifelong discipleship for all ages?' More boldly, perhaps, I assert that the answer is, 'An environment that is intergenerational.' What, then, is meant by 'intergenerational' in the context of Messy Church?

To begin with, being intergenerational is not just about children and young people; it is about people of all ages. It is not primarily about what we do; rather, it is about who we are. It is not something that just happens; it requires intentionality. At the most basic level, being intergenerational is about two or more different generations engaging *relationally* together (some are even using the term 'intergene*rela*tional').[83] Thus, by its very nature, with at least three generations (children, their parents and older leaders/volunteers) often present, Messy Church has the potential to be genuinely intergenerational. However, simply having multiple generations in the same space does not make the experience intergenerational (any more than going to McDonalds makes a person a hamburger or going to church makes a person a Christian). To be an intergenerational experience requires the generations to be genuinely interacting and engaging together – not just predominantly children with children or adults with adults; not just predominantly a small number of adults 'organising' or 'leading' activities for children; not just a parent/carer predominantly engaging with the child/children in their care – but multiple individual interactions across multiple generations.

Being truly intergenerational, however, is much more than our activities and engagement, the things we do. Being intergenerational is also about who we and how we are – our values, our beliefs, our attitudes, our posture in relation to the different generations. In the Messy Church (as well as the inherited church) context, this predominantly plays out in the way we as adults 'see' and relate to children. While being alongside, listening, learning and sharing together are all valuable, being truly intergenerational involves a more comprehensive mutuality (all benefit), equality (all are equally valued) and reciprocity (all give and receive) in relationship. As much as we desire to see children at Messy Church (and in the inherited church) grow and learn and change, how open are we, as adults, to growing, learning and changing as a consequence of our relationships with children? As much as we, as leaders and volunteers, long to see the lives of parents and carers enhanced through their engagement with us, how open are we to being transformed through our relationship with them?

A genuinely intergenerational Messy Church is not something that just happens. It requires intentionality. It requires leadership that has a focus on curating Messy Church as an intergenerational experience. It requires leaders who cultivate values, attitudes and behaviours that enhance intergenerational engagement. It requires modelling and deliberate action on the part of leaders and volunteers. For optimal growth as all-age discipleship communities, Messy Church leaders need to be intentional in developing their understanding and practice of ministry that is truly intergenerational.

By way of summary so far, we have a big-picture understanding of Messy Church as an all-age discipleship community in which the five core values are lived out in every aspect of its life. We have discipleship understood as an intentional orienting towards Jesus that involves following, learning and embodied action. We have an intergenerational environment considered fundamental to lifelong discipleship. There is one more significant piece to explore before we consider a framework for all-age discipleship in the local Messy Church context – the importance of contextualisation.

Central to the phenomenal uptake of Messy Church around the world is the emphasis placed on contextualisation. Messy Church has flourished across such a range of communities, denominations and countries. This is a consequence of the emphasis placed on taking the local context seriously. Messy Church is not a colonising cookie-cutter approach to ministry that is simply rolled out. Instead, listening to the local community is a vital part of the Messy Church discernment process. Any local Messy Church needs to take into account, and allow itself to be shaped by, its specific context – the community it is seeking to engage, the uniqueness of the local church community and the church tradition/denomination in which it sits. Similarly, I suggest that when it comes to discipleship there needs to be similar contextualisation. Just as there is no one-size-fits-all way of being Messy Church (even though each Messy Church shares the same core values), there is no one-size-fits-all expression of Messy discipleship (even though each Messy Church places a high priority on it). Each local Messy Church needs to do the work of contextualising its understanding and expression of discipleship in the light of the specific context in which it is placed.

Challenging though it may be, it is important that Messy Churches take the time to discern, describe, design and develop their approach to discipleship. Close attention needs to be given to their emphasis on all-age discipleship.

The task of **discernment** needs to take into account the tradition/denomination in which the Messy Church sits, the way discipleship is understood by the local church leadership and the nature of the local community being engaged. This discernment seeks a common mind as to how discipleship is to be understood in the local context.

The task of **description** is to identify what discipleship might look like in the specificity of the local Messy Church. The practices, behaviours and actions that arise from the discerned understanding of discipleship need to be clearly described

The task of **design** is to first imagine, and then establish, processes that will encourage the identified practices, behaviours and actions. Particularly important to the design element is the integration of discipleship processes into the whole life of the Messy Church. Such integration of processes needs to foster the expression of discipleship individually, as households and as a whole Messy Church community.

The task of **development** is to focus on the implementation of the agreed processes, monitoring the progress, reviewing the outcomes and adjusting the processes as required.

Rather than the pressure of doing all of the above from scratch, which can sound daunting, there are many discipleship frameworks available that can be adapted to the all-age context of Messy Church. For example, the Here2Stay approach[84] is proving very popular in Australia and New Zealand. There is the Holy Habits approach,[85] which is growing in popularity in the United Kingdom. The advice I often give to churches is that, up to a point, it is more important to adopt an intentional approach and commit to it for an extended period of time than to agonise over which one to choose. Whether you embrace either of these frameworks, use another of your choosing or develop your own, it is vital that it is contextualised to your unique circumstances.

To assist in this overall task of determining and implementing an integrated approach to all-age discipleship, I would also like to offer the model of all-age discipleship CARE – where C is for common understanding, A is for aligned practices, R is for relational emphasis and E is for embedded intergenerationality. Whichever framework is adopted for all-age discipleship and however it is adapted, my suggestion is that these four elements need to be incorporated in the actual processes.

Common understanding, once discerned and agreed upon for the context, needs to be clearly articulated and consistently communicated. It includes not just what is believed about discipleship and how it might be described, but also practically what it looks like. For example, a Messy Church can develop an infographic that highlights five key discipleship practices that it seeks to encourage. Posters of the infographic can be displayed around the space where the Messy Church regularly gathers. Copies of the infographic can be placed in the welcome packs provided to new households. Images from the infographic can be used as visual prompts when a particular practice is being modelled, such as prior to exploring a Bible passage during a Messy celebration time.

Aligned practices refers to the need for the identified, described and modelled practices to be broadly implementable as individuals, households and whole communities. Ideally, different practices need to be integrated as part of a coherent whole rather than being implemented in isolation. For example, a Messy Church can encourage engagement with social justice – perhaps with regard to climate justice. In the activities time, there can be an art project that the whole Messy Church community contributes to. The finished product can then be prominently displayed for other users of the space shared by Messy Church to see. A Messy Church at home resource can be provided to encourage specific action for households. Pro-forma letters that are age-sensitive[86] can be made available for individuals to send to their local Member of Parliament.

Relational emphasis draws upon an understanding that the living out of discipleship through action is intrinsically connected to relationship: relationship with God (as individual, household and community), relationship with God's world (as individual, household and community) and relationship with God's purposes (as individual, household and community). For example, an additional further relational dimension can be added to common practices of prayer. As part of encouraging individuals in prayer, a Messy Church can implement a system of prayer partners or prayer triplets (taking into account appropriate safeguarding practices) that connects people of different generations. As part of encouraging households in prayer, a Messy Church can promote the idea of nearby households regularly partnering together for a prayer walk around their local community. As part of encouraging a Messy Church community as a whole in prayer, a Messy Church can enter into a relationship with another Messy Church that includes a commitment to intentionally pray for one another as whole communities.

Embedded intergenerationality calls for the intergenerational dimension to be a growing part of who we are as individuals and community, as well as in what we do as individuals and as a community. It is especially important that this element is understood, modelled and intentionally cultivated by all those who contribute to the leadership of a Messy Church. Given that embedded intergenerationality will be a new concept for many people, I will take the opportunity to expand on it just a little more. I will also suggest one practical way forward in relation to the leadership of a local Messy Church.

Remembering that while the mere presence of multiple generations does not make an activity intergenerational, nevertheless at least two generations need to be present for such activity to be potentially intergenerational. Thus, a good first step to becoming more intergenerational is to look for more opportunities to proactively bring together people of different ages. Once people of different generations are together, then the possibility of genuine intergenerational relationship – marked by mutuality, equality and reciprocity – becomes real. One especially fruitful zone for this in the context of Messy Church is that of leadership.

When you think about it, most activities in Messy Church have five phases for leaders to consider – planning, preparing, presenting, participating and appraising. Taking the Messy celebration as an example, at some point there is planning, in which an overall shape and direction is set. There is preparation of the specific celebration time and the elements within it. During the celebration time, the individual components will be presented and participated in. At some later point, the celebration will be appraised with a view to affirming what went well and wondering what might have been done differently. Similarly, by way of further example, these same five phases could be applied to an individual component, such as a time of prayer, within the Messy celebration time. Each of these five phases provides the opportunity to be more intergenerational.

Depending on where you are starting from, your next step with regard to embedding intergenerationality will be different. Thus, it is important to identify your starting point. One way to do this would be to map your current reality. Again taking the example of the Messy celebration time and trying to keep things fairly simple, you might like to jot down how many different generations are typically involved in each of the individual phases. Focus particularly on the planning, preparing, presenting and appraising phases. Depending on what you notice, your first challenge might be to intentionally increase the number of generations in one of the phases. You can do this by proactively identifying and inviting an extra person or two to engage with that phase (by way of a side note, you might also want to consider the place of participation in each of these phases within your overall all-age discipleship framework). Next steps, depending on your discernment, might include repeating the process for a different phase or working at deepening the level of intergenerational engagement within that phase. When you are feeling bold enough, you could then proceed with the mapping, noticing and intentionally increasing embedded intergenerationality exercises across other aspects of your Messy Church.

This chapter is an invitation to Messy Churches specifically (and all churches generally) to discern, describe, design and develop their uniquely contextualised approach to discipleship with all ages. It is an encouragement to embrace a framework of all-age disciple-ship CARE – common understanding, aligned practices, relational emphasis, embedded intergenerationality – that can be lived out by individuals, households and Christian communities. It considers the flourishing of an intergenerational environment as foundational to lifelong discipleship. It understands discipleship as including an orientation towards Jesus that involves following, learning and living in ways that accord with Jesus' example. It presents Messy Church as an all-age discipleship community in which the core values of all-age, celebration, Christ-centred, creativity and hospitality are deeply embedded in every aspect of its being. It shares a vision for Messy Churches as communities of all ages growing in their following of Jesus together. It seeks to inspire a passion and provide a pathway for growing discipleship. It arises from a longing to see more disciples of all ages and more communities living out discipleship in response to God's gracious invitation to abundant life.

7

Creativity

Sandy Brodine

Sandy Brodine is a minister of the word in the Banyule Network of Uniting Church, Australia. She is responsible for four emerging faith communities, including two Messy Churches. She has a passion for creative worship and for helping new disciples grow imaginatively and strongly in faith. She lives with her husband, daughter and two dogs in Mitcham, Victoria.

To understand why creativity is so important to growing a robust faith, we need look no further than Jesus and the way he taught his disciples. Rather than a dusty, dry, 'fill in the worksheet and give me the right answers' approach, Jesus took his disciples with him on the road. He showed them how he engaged with people and helped them to understand who he was. He sent them out in small groups on their own to try out their new skills. And he told them stories: perplexing, odd, complicated stories – stories that could be understood in more than one way.

How effective was this creative discipleship strategy of Jesus? Well, the disciples scratched their heads and asked lots of questions. They were often perplexed. But Jesus had captured their imaginations – and he gave them things to try out, long before they could be considered competently ready. They failed regularly. And in this 'playing' at being disciples, they learned. So when Jesus returned to the Father, this motley band of former fishermen and tax collectors were as ready as they could be to disciple and form the faith of others.

Those who choose to follow Jesus, to become disciples in every age, need to find ways to wrestle with these odd and perplexing stories. The reason for this is that following Jesus is not just a simple, one-step process of believing; it is all about being formed in the likeness of Jesus. Andrew Roberts, in his book *Holy Habits*, sets out the goals of discipleship in a simple and straightforward way. He points out that God's mission 'in a nutshell is about the Good News of the Kingdom of God'. Disciples, therefore, are those who are charged with the work of bringing about the kingdom, that is, with transforming the world: 'Transformed into a place where no child is hungry, where no woman is abused. A place where people live in peace. A place of laughter and love, of generosity and grace. A place where God's creation is treated with care and respect and God himself is honoured and worshipped.'[87] In order to bring about such transformation, a lifelong journey of faith formation, of growing to be more Christlike, is necessary. In order to do the work of Christ, disciples need to be formed deeply in the habits of prayer and Bible reading, hospitality and generosity. We need to be formed and informed by the holy scriptures, and creativity and imagination are central to this process of disciple-making.

Creativity, telling stories, play, exploring, wondering, making mistakes, trying again – all of these things are key elements of the way Jesus discipled his followers. So, of course, they are the keys to helping others to get to know Jesus and to follow him. It's no great surprise that these are the main elements that go into building a creative set of Messy Church activities to help disciples of all ages and stages grow in their journeys of following Jesus.

The inclusion of creativity as one of the core values of Messy Church, therefore, ought hardly to be surprising. Creativity and encouraging a theological imagination have been a central part of discipleship formation throughout Christian history. Paintings by early Christians in the catacombs underneath Rome show Christians wrestling with the questions of who Jesus is and what it means to follow him. Indeed, artists have been helping people to wonder about these questions for thousands of years. Likewise, musicians, writers, poets, playwrights, architects, church designers and many others have used their creative talents to help other people get to know Jesus, to encourage wondering and to help people think deeply about what it means to follow Jesus.

What of theologians and biblical scholars, then? Is creativity a core part of thinking theologically, or of studying the Bible? When speaking about how he reads the biblical text, Rowan Williams says: 'My aim in reading is not to find instructions, but to open myself to "God's world" – to the landscape of God's action and the rhythms of life lived in God's presence.'[88] Being open to the text involves bringing all of the creative and wondering powers of one's mind to the text – being open to the possibility that we might discover something new and surprising, or indeed that the text might change us into something new.

A note of caution, however: this 'performative view' of the task of biblical scholarship and of theology, as Nicholas Lash describes it, is not about creatively changing the text, which is not a work of fiction but contains elements of the truth about God. As Lash puts it:

> The New Testament texts do not simply give symbolic narrative expression to certain fundamental and persuasive features of the human drama… They also express their authors' confidence in one man in whom the mystery of divine action is seen to have been embodied and disclosed.[89]

The creative performance of scripture – the act of engaging with it, of stepping inside it and inhabiting it so that it may change us – requires some critical reading and thinking skills, and some depth of scholarship. As Lash points out, in order to perform Shakespeare or play a work of music by Beethoven, some sort of deeper knowledge is required. This is the fine line those of us who develop activities for Messy Church must walk, as we attempt to create activities and experiences to help disciples to grapple with the Bible and their faith in our Messy Churches: helping all people who are forming as disciples to respond creatively to the text and question it robustly, while at the same time maintaining the integrity of the truth to which the text itself points, Jesus Christ.

Employing the creative-enquiry approaches of science in Messy Church

Creativity is not just important in the spheres of theology and spiritual formation. It would have been impossible for many, if not all, of the developments of modern science to occur without the creative impulse. Albert Einstein famously said, 'I am enough of an artist to draw freely upon my imagination. Imagination is more important than knowledge. Knowledge is limited. Imagination encircles the world.' The development of Messy Science has been an attempt to encourage Messy Churches to pick up the creative skills used in scientific enquiry, to help disciples develop a robust, inquisitive faith.

In the Banyule Network of Uniting Churches, where the two Messy Churches I lead reside, we are fortunate to have not one but three professors of various scientific disciplines who have been keen to work with us at including the creative skills scientists employ into our Messy Science sessions. Of his work as a professor of zoology, Mike Clarke says:

A scientist's goal is to strive to get a truer and truer understanding of how the world really works. Replacing one idea, hypothesis or theory with an even better one, as we inch slowly closer to the truth about how the world works. Finding new ways to test our hunches (hypotheses) requires *great creativity*! You don't get scientific breakthroughs and revolutions by simply doing what has always been done before. As a scientist you are constantly searching for creative new ways to view a problem, in the hope that it might lead to new insights into how the world really works.[90]

We have been blessed to be able to develop Messy Science sessions along with professional scientists who take both their faith and their work as scientists seriously. Mike and others have encouraged us to use science experiments not just as object lessons, but as ways to encourage children and adults to enquire deeply about the world around them. This in turn creates an environment where it is safe for disciples to ask questions of their faith in a robust and resilient manner.

When it comes to teaching children about the nature of science and faith, I try to highlight five things, depending on age:

a) the extraordinary universe God has created is wonderful, complex and knowable.

b) great creativity is needed by scientists to understand the extraordinary universe God has created.

c) you can be a scientist and at the same time be a Christian.

d) science addresses HOW questions, and faith addresses WHY questions. While BOTH are really important, answering the HOW question does not answer the WHY question.[91]

I have seen this approach at work in the life of my own daughter, who has a deeply enquiring mind. About 18 months ago, prior to one of our Messy Science sessions, my daughter, then aged seven, informed me that she could no longer believe in God, because 'of the Big Bang'. If the scientific explanation she had been taught at school was true, then God could not be, she reasoned. We had discussed this, and I helped her to think about the different kinds of questions science and faith wrestled with. I encouraged her to ask questions and to talk to people she respected at church and school about it. Just recently, a year and a half later, after hearing stories at Messy Church and engaging with people she trusts, she informed me that she does believe in God, and explained how she had come to this conclusion. Who knows what other hurdles she will face in her faith development, but certainly this creative-thinking approach has helped her to come to an answer which is satisfying to her now nine-year-old mind.

Educational theory and Messy Church

Important tools for Messy Churches can be found among critical thinking and enquiry-based learning models. Many Messy Church practitioners will be familiar with the Godly Play method, developed by Jerome Berryman, whose story-based approach and wondering questions draw heavily on the work of Maria Montessori. Early childhood models of enquiry-based play and sensory play are also helpful tools to have in mind when developing Messy Church activities. Again, these encourage wondering and imaginative engagements with elements of the story or perhaps with spiritual disciplines, such as prayer.

Using a model like Bloom's Taxonomy[92] can help Messy Church leaders to think about whether they are creating tasks which will simply develop a lower-order skill, such as 'remembering' the story or names of characters in a story. Instead, we want to create activities that will help disciples to apply their knowledge of the story to their lives or to use even higher-order thinking skills, like analysing, evaluating and creating, in order to, in Rowan Williams' words, step inside a story and inhabit it. We want people to ask the 'Why?' questions of faith.

Another educational theory useful for Messy Church is Gardner's Theory of Multiple Intelligences,[93] which suggests that every learner learns in different ways. As we develop our Messy Church programme, I try to ensure there is a range of activities which allow participants to engage using the full range of skills, including kinaesthetic (touch or movement based), visual, auditory, verbal-linguistic, musical-rhythmic, interpersonal, intrapersonal, naturalistic (nature based) and existential (spiritual). Hopefully across the range of crafts and activities offered at Messy Church, each person will find a creative way to engage with the story that will fire their imaginations and help them grow as disciples of Jesus.

Other educational models, such as Edward de Bono's Six Thinking Hats,[94] will also help Messy Church leaders think about ways that disciples can engage thoughtfully and critically with the biblical narrative.

You don't need a degree in education to make use of these theories. There are many video clips online which will give you a simple introduction to some of them, so that you can develop a range of creative ways for new disciples of every age to deeply engage with the biblical text and to grow.

Finally, it is worth ensuring that there are activities for people in different emotional states: something quiet that can be done on one's own for the introvert who needs some space or for the person who likes to process on their own. You might like to offer storybooks, preferably on the theme of the day, for families who need to encourage some quiet time for a particular child. Create sensory-appropriate activities for children who need those, alongside boisterous and noisy gross-motor activities for people who prefer to engage in that way.

What kinds of creative activities will help to grow disciples of all ages at Messy Church?

Include open-ended, 'wondering' table questions

Many of us include a question or 'something to think about' to go on the table. When devising the questions, try to include ones that encourage wondering or open discussion around the table, rather than simplistic or 'right' answers which show someone has remembered facts about a story.

Include collaborative art activities

For example, make a large collage or group painting that can be used as a tablecloth for Communion or dinner (perhaps on calico or an old sheet) or a large piece of paper that can become a focus for prayers or part of a prayer activity in worship. Creating a piece of art together encourages conversation and sharing of ideas among participants of all ages – an opportunity for people to explore the story or theme for the day in all sorts of different ways – and enables participants to imagine themselves in the story and to make connections about following Jesus.

During a session on making disciples, we created a big collage painting of the sea. We wondered what it might be like to be out in a little fishing boat on the sea or a big lake. We wondered about what might be scary or exciting in the sea. We wondered what it might be like for fishermen to stop fishing and follow Jesus. We attached a string orange bag to the painting as a fishing net, and during the celebration time we wrote and drew our prayers for people whom we hoped would get to know Jesus and 'get caught in the net'… just like Jesus and his disciples caught people!

Include process activities

In these activities, the process of making is more important than producing a perfect item. A piece of art which is about exploring with paint or some other medium allows the mind to wander creatively and encourages discussion and thinking about the passage or a question in more open or creative ways.

Example 1: Painting on foil with cotton buds. We made 'fishy sea paintings' during a session based on the story of Jesus calming the storm, but it could equally be used for any sea-based story. Because the participants, who were of all ages, were not focusing on making perfect works of art, but were instead enjoying the feeling of the paint on the foil as they talked about the passage, they noticed how the activity freed them up to think differently about the text and to be open to the ideas of the others around the table.

Example 2: Sand, seed and stone designs. I have used different varieties of these with a number of texts – some as large collaborative tasks and others as a personal, reflective activity. They can also be made with stories about 'salt and light' or as a way of exploring concepts of being a Christian community together.

Sensory play activities

Simple kinaesthetic activities can be great for people of all ages, but particularly for small children or those with sensory issues. I try to use sensory elements that are non-toxic and won't cause harm if ingested – for example, oats instead of sand or coloured pasta or rice.

Some examples: washing the farm animals (chocolate pudding and muesli mud) in the context of the story of the lost son, or finger painting with shaving foam as a way of exploring stories of creation. (If you include food dye, it makes beautiful marbled paper for later prayer activities!)

Messy Science and creative thinking

We have had great fun exploring God's creation using the questioning techniques of scientific enquiry at Messy Church. For example, during a session on caring for God's creation, we learned about ways that scientists 'think scientifically' to solve some of the problems we humans have created in the environment. This included watching and wondering about a short video of a Melbourne University Art/Science installation The Urinotron,[95] a project to use the energy in urine into an energy source to charge a mobile phone. We made ecobricks,[96] and each of the scientists did creative experiments with the kids to help them understand ways in which scientists can use their creative talents to solve problems.

Use board games and 'minute to win it' activities

The activity itself doesn't necessarily have to be new and creative – you can use existing activities in innovative ways to help participants make new lateral-thinking connections between concepts and ideas.

For example: Scrabble Worship Words.[97] Following on from this activity at a Holy Habits in Messy Church session, one of our mothers, who is a psychologist, was quite struck by the way in which freeing up an old game from the constraints of the rules allowed her to think more creatively about God and how she understood God. She told me excitedly that this activity was an example of neurogenesis – creating new neural pathways, new creative ways of thinking, allowing her to experience God in new and surprising ways.

To think about

1 Do the activities you use at Messy Church enable participants to learn from one another's creativity?

2 Do the activities you've developed help encourage creative thinking and questioning about faith and discipleship and help grow a robust faith in participants?

3 What kind of thinking skills do the activities you create require? Merely remembering facts about the story – or higher-order analytical and creative skills?

4 Have you included activities to appeal to different kinds of 'intelligences' – to the kinaesthetic, visual, musical and spiritual thinkers in the community?

5 Have you included different modes of engagement: quiet, boisterous, craft, peaceful, gross motor, fine motor, etc.?

8

Hospitality

Jocelyn Czerwonka

 Jocelyn Czerwonka is the Messy Church Coordinator for the Diocese of Waiapu in New Zealand, which covers Bay of Plenty, Hawkes Bay and Eastland in the North Island. She is a member of the New Zealand National Messy Church team which hosted two National Messy Church Conferences in the North and South Islands in February 2020.

Do you ever have a song going around in your head and you can't ignore it? For me over the last few weeks it's been that lovely Fischy Music song that I first heard at the Messy Church International Conference in May 2019 in England: 'Welcome, everybody, it's good to see you here!' After travelling from one side of the world to the other to attend the conference, it was such a joy to hear those words! For some reason I felt at 'home', I felt welcomed, I felt I belonged – it was so good to be there!

I wonder how people feel when they make the journey to Messy Church. If it is their first time, maybe they feel like they are encountering many obstacles, fears and feelings of uncertainty. Maybe they are wondering if this thing called Messy Church is really a place for them to come to or possibly belong. I wonder if they begin to imagine that this could be the beginning of a wonderful journey with God.

Do we welcome people in, roll out the red carpet and believe that, as we do so, lives may be changed, the love of God will be encountered and we are welcoming new people who may be or may yet be amazing disciples of Christ?

For many of us, it will be quite a journey back to Messy Church after encountering lockdown and all that Covid-19 has brought to our world. As I write, New Zealand is looking at moving into 'Level 1', meaning a lot of the restrictions will be lifted but we will still be taking great care. Our teams are starting to reimagine what Messy Church might look like and how it might feel. We've talked about being kind, patient, loving and caring and looking after ourselves, our teams and all people. We are asking ourselves how we do hospitality and rebuild an environment where, with God's help, we can continue to grow disciples. How do we reimagine Messy Church?

A positive outcome of lockdown has been that many more people of all ages have been reached through online Messy Churches, 'Messy Church in a bag' pickups and deliveries, and people reaching out and caring for those in their communities. People who have become disconnected from Messy Church or never even had contact with a Christian community have been reached in some way. It's been an 'upside down' sort of hospitality to that which we have previously been familiar with, where we have taken hospitality to the people in whatever way we have been able, instead of expecting them to come to us. Perhaps Jesus is reminding us about 'being sent out' to the people, perhaps reimagining a church without walls.

As I talked with our cluster of Messy Church leaders in our region recently, we realised how much value there was in remembering those on the edges, who, for whatever reason, find it too hard to get to Messy Church but still long for the contact and sense of belonging to this wonderful family of God's. We realised that even as we get excited about Messy Churches starting again, we must think beyond those who gather 'within the walls' and continue to strive to reach those 'beyond the walls'.

The wonderful value of hospitality may have just become a little bit bigger, a little different, a little more challenging and possibly a little more exciting, as we trust in God to grow disciples through Messy Church in a world that has experienced so much uncertainty due to Covid-19 – a world that has got very messy!

So what is hospitality and why do we think that if we do it well in our Messy Churches we can grow disciples?

Good hospitality always begins with good preparation and that, along with a dedication to 'grow disciples', begins with our Messy Church teams. We can learn much from the book of Acts and the description of the believers forming community:

> All the believers devoted themselves to the apostles' teaching, and to fellowship, and to sharing in meals (including the Lord's Supper), and to prayer… all the while praising God and enjoying the goodwill of all the people. And each day the Lord added to their fellowship those who were being saved.
> ACTS 2:42, 47 (NLT)

Meeting together regularly as teams – praying together, sharing meals and breaking bread together, as the early communities of believers did – will enable us to form community, to hear God's word together and to be more effective in our planning, preparation and discipleship at Messy Church.

We must remember, too, not to allocate 'hospitality' to just our cooks and kitchen helpers. Hospitality is the responsibility of every team member, not just at the table or in the kitchen but in all we do at Messy Church. As a team we must each practise hospitality in whatever our gifts or roles may be. We must be mindful of the needs of all those coming. Knowing about and catering for special needs, such as disabilities and dietary requirements, should be considered. Are we aware of different cultural customs and things we might do that may offend others? For instance, in Maori culture it is offensive to sit on tables, and in many cultures it is offensive to touch a person's head.

Good hospitality also means keeping people safe. We need to ensure health and safety checks are up to date, that people in our teams are vetted, that our buildings and surroundings meet safety standards and that our activities and equipment are safe. Take time also to consider providing an eco-friendly environment and resources, so that we model the importance of caring for all of God's creation.

I will always remember a delightful little girl arriving for the very first time at a 'pop-up' Messy Church we ran after a training day. She was so excited, dressed up for the occasion and bubbling with enthusiasm. When we welcomed her, she announced, 'We've come to make the church *messy*!'

How wonderful! We sometimes need to make the church messy – after all, Jesus did! If we are honest, we are all messy in one way or another. Our lives aren't perfect – we have our ups and downs, and we all fall short in some way or another. But God has called us, we belong to God's family and we are on a journey following Jesus, serving Jesus and wanting to be more like Jesus. So, yes – 'we've come to make the church messy' was a wonderful proclamation from this three-year-old girl.

After Jesus called Levi (Matthew) to follow him, he attended a banquet at Levi's home. The Pharisee's and teachers complained bitterly about Jesus eating with 'such scum'. Jesus responded, saying,

'Healthy people don't need a doctor – sick people do. I have come to call not those who think they are righteous, but those who know they are sinners and need to repent' (Luke 5:30–32, NLT).

That is a mandate to do what Jesus did: welcome with open arms people who some might think will make the church messy!

When our children were young, we lived in a vicarage next to the church. It was a small community, and most of the children walked in little groups to the same school. Behind our house lived a foster family with a rather challenging young boy, whom I will call Johnny (not his real name), who happened to be the same age (five at the time) as our youngest. He adopted us as his second home and family to 'hang out with'. He sometimes came to church and would tell us about his pet lion in his bedroom and so much more. His older foster brothers decided they liked the look of our children's new bikes and one night decided to take them on permanent loan – which Johnny soon told us about.

As a young mum, I was somewhat challenged by this little boy who made himself very much at home, and I wondered if he might be a bad influence on our son. Praying about it one night, I was prompted to read a scripture from Hebrews 13:2: 'Do not forget to show hospitality to strangers, for by so doing some people have shown hospitality to angels without knowing it.'

Could we possibly have been entertaining an 'angel' all this time?

Our hospitality did backfire one more time, when this little 'angel' arrived at our home one day when we were out. Volunteers from our church were working in the vicarage and saw Johnny arrive. Thinking he was one of ours arriving home from school, they took little notice. I was horrified to arrive home and discover this five-year-old was away with the fairies, having polished off the remnants from our wine cooler, left on the bench after a meal with guests the night before. After checking with the Poisons Centre and being reassured he would be okay, I took Johnny home to his foster mum. He couldn't walk a straight line down the road, and the story soon spread around the neighbourhood that little Johnny had got drunk at the vicarage!

I still often think about Johnny today, some 30 years later, and hope and pray that, against the odds, with God's love and mercy, this young man has grown up to know, love and serve God.

I share this story because it's a reminder that we may never know when we are entertaining angels. As the scripture in Hebrews reminds us, we should show 'hospitality to strangers', even if they might challenge us and make our church, our homes or, dare I say it, our reputations messy!

There is a wonderful word from the Maori language: *Manaakitanga*. *Manaakitanga* embraces so much about hospitality and is a central value in Maori culture.

Speaking to much-loved *kaumatua* (Maori elders) in our community, they told me that *manaakitanga* is what hospitality in Messy Church is all about. It is about welcoming people, caring for people and showing kindness and generosity. It is about respecting and supporting one another and sharing love and compassion. *Manaakitanga* is not just about the food that is offered; it is about the whole experience of Messy Church, from the welcome to the times of creativity, the celebration and meeting with Christ, the *karakia* (prayer and giving thanks), the meal, the thanking and appreciation of the cooks and the sending out.

Manaakitanga starts at the gate. The welcome people receive will set the tone for how people will feel as they step into what may be a strange and new environment. Our doors should be open, our welcome area inviting, our hosts friendly and welcoming people, giving out name tags and information to help visitors feel at home. Not only is it good to know visitors' names and where they have come from, but also it is important for those who are welcoming visitors to share their story – who they are, where they are from – and to explain what this place called Messy Church is all about. This is the beginning of building relationship, the beginning of the discipleship journey.

Welcoming people by name

Names are so important. In Isaiah 49:14–16 we read about the people of Jerusalem feeling forgotten and deserted by God, and yet the Lord replies in verse 16, 'I have written your name on the palms of my hands' (NLT).

I am sure there are times in all our lives when we feel forgotten and deserted, whether by God or by the people around us, and particularly as we grapple with what Covid-19 has done to our world. There is something powerful about being 'called by name' and even more so to know that God's love for us is so great that our names are 'written' or 'inscribed' (as some versions say) on the palm of his hands.

We have a lot of homeless people in our city, and for many years our inner-city church ran a drop-in centre and provided a weekly meal. The vicar (who happens to be my husband) was walking through town one day and came across one of the homeless men. He stopped and chatted, as he did on many occasions to the street people, and called this man by his name, Andrew. Towards the end of the conversation, Andrew said, 'Thank you. So many people pass me by and look the other way, but you knew me by name and stopped and chatted, and that means a lot.' Andrew stayed in contact and valued the relationship and friendship that was acknowledged that day.

There is so much to learn from this story. Names are important, and we need to make the effort to learn and remember people's names. Let's not turn the other way when people we struggle with pass us by, but let us acknowledge all people, regardless of race, social standing or lack thereof, and be sure to call them by name. We live in communities where some people struggle to belong, and we can make a difference.

There are two delightful young sisters who come to our Messy Church. They look very much alike and yet have very different personalities. For a long time I would get their names muddled up. They would greet me with such excitement, but if I got their names wrong they would be quite indignant. I very quickly had to sort that out and make a mental note of who was who and ensure I called them by their correct names. Name tags certainly help!

To be known by name is to be acknowledged as an individual, not as a sister of someone, a 'streetie', a problem-child or another grey-haired old lady. To be known by name is to be valued and appreciated for who you are. To be known by name helps us to feel we belong. Learning to pronounce names properly is also extremely important, especially as we welcome people of different cultures and languages.

Seeing, hearing and doing

> There is an expectation among Maori that we learn by 'seeing, hearing and doing'. We 'see' and 'hear' the ways and customs of the people and become involved in the 'doing'.[98]

I wonder if that is our expectation in Messy Church. I wonder if the hospitality we provide allows for people of all ages to 'see' and 'hear' and become involved in the 'doing'. Are we growing disciples through Messy Church? Are they 'seeing' and learning from Christlike actions they see? Are they 'hearing' the love of God through the helpers and leaders at Messy Church? Are we involving all ages, all people and giving them all opportunities to be 'doers' of the faith?

We can learn so much from each other and particularly from other cultures. My friend Mele has shared with me what hospitality means to Pasifika (indigenous peoples of the Pacific Islands) :

> You know you have received Pasifika hospitality when you come away feeling like you've been treated like royalty!

Pasifika hospitality is often portrayed as highly generous, with their ravishing feasts and gifts, colourful and entertaining. Whether it is in the home or in a public setting, no matter the occasion or celebration, hospitality is regarded as an important cultural value and presented at its finest.

Pasifika hospitality is collective. The responsibilities do not depend on just a person or family, but it's a given that it is a shared role and experience. At the heart of it are the values of service and love. We recognised that symbols of dance and song, *talanoa* (sharing of stories), giving of gifts and especially food are common ways we do and create to honour these values. It is also about spiritual significance as well. We give of ourselves, our time and resources to serve others and to build lasting relationships just as Christ exampled and taught us. We take on the understanding that when we bless and love others, we will also be blessed in return.

Pasifika hospitality is never complete until you leave with a parting gift, whether it is in a form of a cultural offering or simply a song sending you best wishes as you go on your way.

I wonder if our Messy Church guests feel treated as royalty.

Table ministry and food

Our *kaumatua* friends sent me this Maori proverb about the sharing of resources: *Nau te rourou, naku te rourou, ka ora te manuhiri* ('With your food basket and my food basket, the guests will have enough').

For some coming to Messy Church, the meal is a bonus, but for many this may be one of the few nutritious meals they have had for some time. The physical nourishment we provide at Messy Church may for some be the start of 'seeing Christ in action' through our efforts. God's provision is evident as teams and communities work together to find healthy food options to fill our baskets and provide nutritious meals to share at Messy Church.

In a small rural town called Putaruru, there is a wonderful Messy Church team which oozes hospitality. Mary, who heads up the team, has lived in the area for many years and knows the community well. The 'seeing', 'hearing' and 'doing' is evident in their ministry, and they recognise each other's gifts and strengths that they can share. This team knows well the concept of preparing a banquet for a 'Messy Church feast', and their actions remind me of Jesus' response to the righteous ones when they asked:

> 'Lord, when did we ever see you hungry and feed you? Or thirsty and give you something to drink? Or a stranger and show you hospitality?…' And the King will say, 'I tell you the truth, when you did it to one of the least of these my brothers and sisters, you were doing it to me!'
>
> MATTHEW 25:37–40, NLT

Mary shares about soup ministry:

> During winter families are asked to bring along a large pot for soup making. We provide all the ingredients for a nutritious soup. Together everyone prepares a large pot of soup to take home. When one eight-year-old girl arrived home with her pot of soup, the rest of her siblings were lined up with their soup bowl and spoon before I had even put the pot of soup on the stove. God constantly reminds me about the importance of hospitality and feeding his people.

Marilyn talks about the importance of circulating and talking to everyone at the tables. Many often comment that they don't eat meals at home this way. What we model at Messy Church can lead to healthier homes and families taking time to sit, eat and talk together. Often children will remind parents to take time to say grace and give thanks for the food. It is important that the Messy Church team mingles with those gathered and not stick to a table of 'us and them'.

Sally shares:

I wanted to role-model a traditional family table setting. Over the years I've learnt the importance of families eating together being one of the easiest ways to create a family life tradition. Creating that special 'together' sense where we give thanks by saying grace, we face one another and we talk about life and school and issues just as it has been done for centuries, around the table.

She continues:

At Messy Church we like to go the extra mile, like one does at Christmas, giving a wow-sense to honour our 'guests' and make the evening special. The table is prepared with nice tablecloths and the cutlery set out. We may use paper doilies in white, gold or silver to decorate, and place messages or some decoration relating to the theme of Messy Church that day. We have water glasses that we place white or coloured paper serviettes in, and water jugs on the table in preference to juice or cordial. The centre of the table can have printouts pertaining to the theme displayed on stands. Sometimes I put balloons on sticks for the wow-factor. Other times little flower arrangements or cafe table clips holding message cards is an option. Hanging colourful bunting makes the room cheery. For a harvest or thanksgiving theme, I've used jars of bottled peaches, and scattered fruit and greenery on tables.

It pays to ask God what he would like you to do, and often little ideas just fall into place. It allows the team to join in together, be creative and go the extra mile for our special guests. There is huge scope for creativity and memorable settings with amazing food served that is nutritious, wholesome and family-oriented. Our church has always had a history of great food and hospitality prior to our Messy Church, so by continuing to offer great home-cooked food for free was important to us to honour our forebears and our guests and our own country's sense of *manaakitanga*. As the many of our families are Maori, this aspect is hugely important. As followers of Christ, it is in our own tradition to offer hospitality, generosity and welcome to our guests by the high quality of the food, the setting, the excitement to prepare it in advance, and to set the room as if Jesus is coming to join in with our families.

In another city, Miriam talks about gathering Messy Church people together after lockdown:

> When cafes were open but we were unable to use the church facilities, I organised a cafe gathering. It was a chance for everyone to see each other after lockdown. People happily gathered there, some at different tables and near the children's play area. It was great to see all ages gathering and talk about possibly starting Messy Church soon. Everyone was pleased to get out and have a coffee together. It wasn't hospitality as we know it, but things are different now.

However we offer hospitality, what is invaluable is the sharing of our stories, the sharing of our faith and the sharing of our lives together. The sharing is also in the 'hearing' of the stories of our guests and the opportunity to invite Jesus into the conversations.

As we reimagine Messy Church after the disruptions of Covid-19, we may need to adapt our ways of doing hospitality and providing *manaakitanga*. With God, there is always a way, and as we pray together and meet together (even if it's online or at a distance), we can still allow God to inspire us with new ways of 'seeing, hearing and doing' Messy Church – and, most importantly, growing disciples. What matters is that Christ is at the centre of it all.

As we move forward, here is another Maori proverb and scripture to leave you with:

Kia kaha, be strong.
Kia mia, be steadfast.
Kia manawanui, be willing.

Be strong and steadfast; have no fear or dread of them, for it is the Lord, your God, who marches with you; he will never fail you or forsake you.

DEUTERONOMY 31:6 (NABRE)

9

Celebration

Martyn Payne

Formerly part of BRF's Messy Church team, Martyn Payne has a background in Bible storytelling and leading all-age worship, and is passionate about the blessing that comes when generations explore faith together.

Playful discipleship in the celebration

'To celebrate' is a very versatile verb! We celebrate a birthday party; we celebrate a life at a funeral; we celebrate a national day with pageantry; we celebrate an achievement with a medal; we celebrate Communion in church; and we celebrate with music, story and prayers in Messy Church. What unites these different celebrations is a sense of occasion where there is togetherness, a shared and joyful experience of thankful remembering and honouring of someone or something.

It's no accident that Messy Church has adopted 'celebration' as one of its five core values, but it is far more than an alternative word for the gathered-worship part of the service. Of course 'the celebration' is commonly used to describe this aspect of Messy Church, but it also sets the tone for the whole experience of coming together as the people of God.

Celebration and the character of God

Celebration captures the truth that, as Christians, we worship a party-throwing God: a God who is like a shepherd rejoicing over finding his wayward sheep; like the woman gathering with her friends to rejoice over the coin she has found; and like the father laying on a feast for his long-lost son. This sense of being honoured, even treated by God as a celebrity in a celebration, should be part of what is happening when we gather as church. And in itself this is both life-giving and life-affirming, particularly in an age when many of us can feel reduced to being a mere statistic and a number. Celebration connects us with a God who loves to celebrate and who, according to the prophets, exults over us 'with loud singing' (Zephaniah 3:17, NRSV) and counts us as his 'treasured possession' (Malachi 3:17; see also Exodus 19:5). 'Celebration' is indeed a rich and meaningful word, but exactly how does a time of gathered celebration help us grow as disciples of Christ?

Traditional discipleship

In more traditional church services, we are used to the sermon as the most obvious and intentional moment of discipleship. This is the 'teaching slot', which at its best opens up the Bible to help us grow in our knowledge of God and challenges us to put our faith into practice. However, beautifully crafted prayers and other parts of a liturgy can also inspire us to a growing commitment to the truth of what we believe, particularly through repetition and habit. The big question, then, is whether Messy Church services, and in particular that gathered moment we call 'the celebration', can equally feed and sustain us on a discipleship journey. Traditional liturgies and sermons are not the norm in Messy Church, so is the discipleship offered less nurturing, even deficient, as a result?

Over many years with the BRF Messy Church team, I took part in hundreds of Messy Church celebrations around the UK, and I have also led a fair few in my time, either at my own Messy Church or as a guest elsewhere. Therefore, in this chapter I'd like to share some of the positive ways discipleship can be accessed in the Messy celebration.

Discipleship through the Bible story

The stories of God and God's people are timelessly fascinating and draw in listeners of all ages. Storytelling was at the heart of Jesus' ministry, and so it is no surprise that Messy Church is inspired and shaped by Bible stories. The best Messy teams do not begin their planning meetings by saying, 'Now, I have come across this great craft activity, how can we include it next time?' Instead, they start with the Bible story, engaging with it for themselves first of all, before imagining creatively how to help their Messy congregation to share in and build upon the things that they have begun to discover.

Bible study has long been one of the main ways in which disciples grow in their faith. It was one of the foundations of the first church in Jerusalem after Pentecost, where we read that 'they devoted themselves to the apostles' teaching' (Acts 2:42, NRSV). The New Testament had not, of course, been written at this stage – those first Christians were in fact in the process of writing it with their lives! They did, however, have the Jewish scriptures – the Old Testament – and they used it both to help them understand what God was doing in their day and to help them pray. This is how they were disciples of God's word, and if we want to be disciples of Jesus, we need to engage with God's word too.

A thread of discipleship

In my experience, Messy Church does this in abundance! Rather than offering a Bible reading followed by a sermon, Messy Church offers over an hour's worth of creative ways to explore the Bible story for each session. At our own Messy Church I am privileged to be part of a team who love the Bible and who feel it is important to personally experience its impact. I hope you can say the same. So when, say, a Messy team member is engaging with children and adults in an experiment about floating items on water at an activity table, it is so natural for that table leader to share his or her testimony of what it means for him or her to 'step out of the boat' and trust in Jesus. What the leader offers is not a sermon, but, when put together with all that is said from all the activity tables, it helps prepare the congregation for the gathered story to come. In Messy Church, no one arrives at the sermon cold. The activities are a way of getting ready as a congregation to explore the story for that day. The depth of such Bible engagement is already obvious.

Telling the story

And then comes the story itself. Now every celebration storyteller has their way of leading this, whether as an impromptu piece of drama with plenty of participation, as a series of simple 3D visuals laid out for all to see, or as pictures and video to help people into the story. The wonderful thing to remember is that God does not have a favourite way for his stories to be told. Whenever a faithful follower is prepared to stand up and share the good news, God is at work. What is most important is that the story comes from the heart and that everyone is given the opportunity to enjoy the story together, to wonder about that story and to find their own personal response to it. It's about how we work out the story in our own lives, and for that we simply need the invitation to step into a story that has been faithfully told.

Becoming Messy disciples

The Holy Spirit is our inspiration in all this. It is the Spirit who takes the words of God and the stories of Jesus and breathes life into them for each one of us. For this to happen, we need to give the Holy Spirit space to work. And this means not only covering the whole experience in prayer, but also being open as a storyteller to be a listener and a learner along with the congregation. This is how Jesus taught his disciples. There were questions and answers; there was laughter and conversation; there was repetition as well as space to think.

Christians have always believed that the stories in the Bible are mysteriously God-breathed, as Paul describes them in his letter to Timothy (2 Timothy 3:16) and as such are a tool for our discipleship, teaching us more about God, more about God's love and more about ourselves and who we are meant to be. The best celebrations that I have attended have given space for God. The team did not see the Messy celebration as the highpoint of their Messy Church – the moment when the real God stuff happens! – but rather as the moment that draws together the threads of all the activities on the Bible story and then moves everyone forward into new ideas and thoughts about the story, which can spill over into the mealtime, into their homes and into the week ahead. These are Messy celebrations that do not try to provide all the answers but leave us with plenty of questions and new thoughts to pursue. Once again, this is how Jesus did discipleship with his first followers, who were so often left puzzled, challenged and asking further questions.

All-age discipleship

There is one final and vital dimension to all of this for Messy Church. This Bible-story discipleship happens when different generations are together. Now this is distinctly countercultural as far as traditional church services are concerned. In most churches still, when it comes to learning, congregations prefer to default either to speaking to one group only while others spectate, or they separate off into different age groups. This approach to learning may be appropriate for the secular curriculum, but in church we are following a spiritual curriculum. We are exploring and experiencing Christian discipleship, and contributions to this can come from any age group. Indeed, it is often the very young and very old who offer the most on this discipleship journey together.

Whenever I visit a Messy Church, there is for me a special excitement that, at last, I am stepping into something close to the sort of church that Jesus hoped for. What do I mean? Well, when he talked about discipleship with a gathered group of grown-ups around him, his first act was to invite a child and put her in their midst (Matthew 18:1–5). Hers wasn't a token presence; it was far more. That child, Jesus said, was the model for discipleship for entering the kingdom of God, showing us all the way to become the best disciples possible. Messy Church is church with children in the midst – an all-age place of discipleship that takes those words of Jesus seriously.

Discipleship through prayer

A second common feature in the celebration at Messy Church is prayer. Once again this is something that need not be confined to the gathered moment called 'the celebration', and indeed many Messy Churches are now including a creative prayer station as one of their activity tables. Even so, congregational prayer still has its place and, I believe, a distinct role in helping us become disciples of Jesus.

Corporate prayer has long been recognised as vital for Christian discipleship. Spending time together with God, both listening and interceding for others, helps Christians grow in their faith. But prayer, while perhaps being the most natural thing to do – the cry of our heart – can also be the hardest spiritual discipline to learn and exercise.

Developing the habit of prayer

What helps, for most of us, is being given words and patterns to use that can become central to our lives. Jesus recognised this when he gave his first disciples the words of the Lord's Prayer (Matthew 6:9–13). There was also his own example of praying early in the morning and late into the night, which must have been an inspiration for his first followers. As with devotion to the apostles' teaching, 'the prayers' are specifically mentioned as foundational for the life of the first church in Acts 2:42 (NRSV). The fact that it is referred to as 'the prayers' suggests that this was not only a regular feature but that it embraced different sorts of praying as well. There were, for example, the three-times-a-day prayers in the temple, as well as 'anytime praying', as happened when they faced the crisis of Peter and John being arrested and later the threat to Peter's life.

For me, one of the most important purposes of the prayers in a Messy Church celebration is their role as an example – a good habit to be absorbed almost unconsciously. I am always sad when prayer is reduced to just a few rushed words from the leader, squeezed in between the end of the talk and the start of the meal. This is to miss the discipleship potential of prayer for a congregation which is typically new to church and to prayer.

Types of Messy prayers

In contrast, some Messy Churches have developed their own Messy Church prayers or regularly use the Lord's Prayer with actions.[99] I would also recommend prayers based on what has just been shared in the Bible story, using simple actions and repeated words that are easy to memorise and which involve participation. Even the use of signposted silences can be really helpful for those setting out on the adventure of prayer. For many at Messy Church, prayer is something very new. This needs to be recognised if we are to make disciples, giving as much attention to corporate prayer as is afforded to presenting the Bible story or choosing the song.

Short, regular prayers

Liturgical prayers in traditional services offer patterns to follow and memorable words and responses to use, and this too can be something Messy Church can emulate. Repeated words become internalised and develop into handholds for faith for people taking their first steps as Christian disciples. Why not build into the celebration memorable one-line prayers based on scripture, such as: 'Lord, teach us to pray' (Luke 11:1); 'Lord, help us to believe' (Mark 9:24); 'Speak, Lord, your servant is listening' (1 Samuel 3:9); and 'Lord, we do not know what to do, but our eyes are on you' (2 Chronicles 20:12)? Another such prayer that has been used down the Christian centuries is a prayer asking for forgiveness, known as the Jesus Prayer, taken from Luke's record of the parable of the Pharisee and the tax collector (Luke 18:9–14): 'Lord, have mercy on me, a sinner.' Maybe there is a place for a Messy version of this for the 21st century: 'Please help me, Lord, I'm always messing up.'

Many Messy Churches are already doing this, using language that is accessible to all ages and idioms that are recognisable today. Because they are used regularly, they stick and can help shape lifelong habits of gratitude in prayer. Perhaps the most popular Messy prayer is the Messy Grace, with actions.[100] This takes Paul's trinitarian prayer from 2 Corinthians 13:14 and turns it into a parting blessing for us all that can hold us safe on our discipleship journey, as well as expressing the very heart of what we believe about God.

Discipleship through singing

That leaves one final element to the gathered moment in Messy Church, namely the singing. There is no doubt about the power of singing together. Music can not only articulate deep emotions and express the mystery of faith, but words and music combined are definitely one of the best ways to commit its truths to our hearts and minds. The challenge comes when we start discussing tastes in

Christian worship music and particularly what works or does not work in a Messy Church context. I have to confess I have usually held my peace on my visits regarding the choice of songs!

There are varieties of music

In an effort to make the singing accessible, many Messy Churches have tended to default to what are generally regarded as children's songs. Others are strong advocates of the latest worship music, while some stick to short, simple choruses, recognising that many of the families who come are unused to singing about faith in any shape or form. Yet others have created their own songs or are passionate supporters of this or that musician or band. For me, what matters most is what is being internalised through the singing, both about God and about how we express our faith. This applies whatever choice of songs or preference in music we have. So this is a key question to ask: will the words and the tunes be those that root the singers in truths that will hold them on their Christian journey ahead? I think back to the choruses I learnt when I first became a Christian, and I know that in times of crisis, doubt or fear, it has been those words and their simple tunes that have come to mind and brought me back home to God again. Thinking of this, it is worth looking carefully at the words of the songs we choose to check that they have this lasting dimension.

As a rule, such hymns, worship songs or choruses – call them what you like – should be about God and God's character, use familiar language and images, and have tunes that are easy to pick up. And if you do choose to have actions, they should be meaningful ones, not over-complicated or too childish and ideally bearing some relation to recognised sign language so that they are accessible to those with additional needs. Songs play a very important role in discipleship, and a small, carefully chosen set of songs, sung regularly, will help people hold on to the faith they are finding in Messy Church.

Conclusion

Messy Churches vary tremendously. Some, to be honest, are not far removed from the after-school clubs or Sunday schools from which they have emerged, while others are simplified versions of the old family service but without any liturgy. Still others – and I have been privileged to visit many – are determined to be intentional disciple-making *churches*, where the team sees what happens within the two hours of their Messy Church as an opportunity not only to talk about faith for the first time but also to help people grow in that faith for the time to come. Of course, there is a role for extras and add-ons to support Messy Church discipleship, but we should not lose sight of the opportunity to let every part of a basic Messy Church offer creative tools for discipleship, a discipleship that uses all the senses and engages young and old in shared conversations and learning together. We know that people are coming to faith through Messy Church, and there is no reason why that same context cannot be the place where they go on to grow in their love and service of God.

Conclusion

Lucy Moore

Looking to the present and future

In the introduction, we considered the past and present. If there's such a thing as an outroduction, this is the opportunity to consider the present and the future.

Most specifically, we can look forward to the research that Church Army's Research Unit is completing on discipleship in Messy Church – Deepening Discipleship. Building on *Playfully Serious*, Deepening Discipleship will have been tested in the flames of oppression, frustration, wilderness and loss. What comes out will be gold.

More generally, Messy leaders can be reminded of a great deal of wisdom by the story featured in the September 2020 edition of *Get Messy!* – that of David and Goliath. It's a poignant one for me, as it was one of the final Messy Church sessions at which I helped lead in my local church, before we moved to a new home many miles away. It was also the first time our little Messy Church met face to face again after five months of Covid-induced 'Messy Church in a bag' and Messy Church online. The concept of feeling very vulnerable in the face of a vicious, well-armed and apparently unbeatable enemy is apposite. (And our masks, we discovered, with their elastic earloops, looked very like David's sling.)

What are the giants that loom over us, hurling ridicule and making us feel inadequate? What are the real threats and opportunities for this tiny community of Messy Church within the wider community of God's people? And how do they relate to discipleship?

Complacency

One danger is the self-congratulatory state of mind that a shepherd boy of a lesser calibre than David might have been tempted to wallow in. It would be very easy to feel smug and complacent after knocking the stuffing out of a wolf in your own little valley, without realising that in the next valley the fate of the whole nation was at stake. Messy Church is doing a grand job, and its local leaders and teams are heroes, but let's always be on the lookout for the bigger opportunity, the wider horizon, the next frontier. Let's tell each other, 'Well done! We did that well!', and then point each other towards tomorrow's challenge, for which yesterday's challenge prepared us beautifully. Will we need to face the giants of social injustice? Discrimination against age, gender or race? Unjust structures or outdated practices in the church itself? Oppression in any of its forms? Or perhaps Messy Church is uniquely placed to let the child amble into the midst of adult affairs and demonstrate alternative solutions to apparently impenetrable problems. One aspect of discipleship must be that, by definition, disciples are always learning, standing on what has been learned and stepping out towards the new opportunity.

Being risk averse

One thing I've noticed, as I've become a mother and got older, is that I am nowhere near as risk-happy as I was in my teens and early 20s. I've lost that attitude that the young David had, of seeing an opportunity or problem and throwing myself in without considering the consequences or cost. Risk assessments have entered my life. I'm more aware of all that could go horribly wrong. To my horror, I'm sometimes prouder to be the one to say, 'But wait! Have we considered…?', than to be the one who says, 'Let's do it!' I wonder if Jesus chose to go to the cross at such an early age because it would have got harder with every passing decade. Because Messy Church is made up of such a wide range of ages of people, it's a movement that can choose to stay risk-happy, adventurous, unafraid, daring, bold, intrepid, heroic, undaunted, indomitable, spirited, resolute, reckless – in fact, all the adjectives we apply to young David, despite the passing years. Or we can be like Saul's army in the face of their admittedly very real threat: calculating, timid, risk-averse, petrified, cautious, reluctant, cagy, nervous, hesitant, protective. Being an Anglican myself within an even more glorious Messy mix of denominations, I would, of course, advocate for a happy medium between the two. But the small boy's voice of courageous protest must always be louder than the patronising laughter of his elder brothers from their safe army camp. Our discipleship journey as a movement reflects and shapes the individual discipleship journeys of those who belong to that movement. Looking to the future, can we stay edgy, venturesome and courageous, even to the point of foolishness, in order to encourage everyone Messy, young or old, to be the same and to expect a journey with God to be a risky one?

Size matters

The story of David and Goliath is classically the power of the small in God's ecology. Little David, one small boy, five stones and a sling, who conquers the giant in the power of the Lord. The little boy in John's gospel, with his five loaves and two fish, who conquers the hunger of thousands in the power of Jesus. The tiny Christian community of Acts 4, who recognised Jesus as the cornerstone, whose words and courage meant 5,000 people becoming believers in one day in the power of the Spirit. David is part of a biblical motif of the small, apparently hopeless, ridiculous, risible offering that nonetheless, through the power of the unstoppable God, reverses a desperate situation or releases the working of an amazing miracle.

Looking to the future, Messy leaders can take hope and confidence in this godly principle and believe in the power unleashed when a person of faith offers themselves and their resources, without reservation, into the hands of the living God. Like David, there will be those supposedly on our side who oppose us, whether that's someone on the church council at a local level or someone influential and 'important' from a churchmanship that dismisses Messy Church as inferior and inadequate. But, like David, we can stay true to the most pressing concern, despite being a small and apparently insignificant player. For him, this was the survival of a nation; for us, it's the salvation of each new generation. Discipleship is about pressing on towards the goal, undeterred by obstacles. If we can model this as a movement, it will be a trait passed on to the disciples made though Messy Church.

We could draw out other parallels between David's example and Messy discipleship. There's David's refusal to put on armour that simply didn't fit and the challenge to Messy Church to find new ways to worship that fit not just the old but also the young, not just those brought up in church but also those new to it. We could think about the way David was on the run for a large part of his life (and how it was when he settled down to palace life that he fell into trouble with temptation) and the challenge to Messy Church to stay mobile, flexible and able to respond to changing circumstances. There's the way David had a vibrant relationship with the living God but didn't hesitate to bend religious rules when the need arose and the challenge to Messy Church to put a relationship with Jesus first and the relationship with inherited religious structures in second place when there is a conflict of interest. There's the simple challenge to remember that children play a key role in God's purposes if the well-equipped, well-structured, well-ordered adult world makes space for them. Actually, even if it doesn't.

The kingdom David eventually established reflected his values and started to grow a people who shared those values, then helped shape the kingdom in their turn. The early church's values (Acts 2:42–47) shaped the people who belonged to it, and they in turn shaped the church as it developed. We look forward to seeing how the five values of Messy Church continue to shape people of all ages, who in turn shape the church to which they belong, to become ever-more hospitable, even more creative, bubbling over with still more celebration and providing ever-more unignorable examples of why intergenerational church is valuable. But most of all, with every passing generation, we long, by God's grace and in the power of the Holy Spirit, to become ever-more centred around Jesus and shaped by him.

Notes

1 Church Army's Research Unit, *Playfully Serious: How Messy Churches create new space for faith* (Church Army, 2019): **churcharmy.org/Publisher/File.aspx?ID=225713**.

2 George Lings, *The Day of Small Things: An analysis of fresh expressions of church in 21 dioceses in the Church of England* (Church Army, 2016), p. 41: **churcharmy.org/Publisher/File.aspx?ID=204265**.

3 For the Messy Churches who ticked this fxC type only, across the 21 dioceses, 712 Messy Churches were listed for us to follow up, and only 302 met our fxC indicators (42%) and were included in *The Day of Small Things*.

4 Church Army's Research Unit, *Painting with Numbers* (Church Army, 2019): **churcharmy.org/Publisher/File.aspx?ID=224311**

5 See *Painting with Numbers*, p. 7 for the number of Messy Churches in our sample begun each year.

6 *Painting with Numbers*, pp. 6–14.

7 Church Army's Research Unit, *Managing the Mess* (Church Army, 2019): **churcharmy.org/Publisher/File.aspx?ID=224307**

8 Church Army's Research Unit, *What Goes On Inside* (Church Army, 2019): **churcharmy.org/Publisher/File.aspx?ID=224305**.

9 The full list of outputs is available here: **churcharmy.org/Groups/319979/Church_Army/web/What_we_do/Research_Unit/Playfully_Serious/Playfully_Serious.aspx**.

10 Church Army's Research Unit, *Discipleship Definitions* (Church Army, 2019): **churcharmy.org/Publisher/File.aspx?ID=224306**.

11 *Painting with Numbers*, p. 16.

12 Lings, *The Day of Small Things*, pp. 88–89.

13 *Managing the Mess*, p. 31.

14 **gov.uk/government/statistics/english-indices-of-deprivation-2015**; see *Painting with Numbers*, pp. 6, 16.

15 Scott Peck, *The Different Drum* (Arrow, 1990).

16 *Managing the Mess*, p. 42.

17 *Painting with Numbers*, p. 18.

18 *Painting with Numbers*, pp. 30.

19 *Painting with Numbers*, pp. 40–41 – which includes the percentages for fxC MES and outreach MES.

20 Alan Roxburgh, *Missionary Congregation, Leadership and Liminality* (Continuum, 1997).

21 Gerald Arbuckle, *Refounding the Church: Dissent for leadership* (Geoffrey Chapman, 1993), p. 120.

22 *Painting with Numbers*, p. 15. These attendance figures include team.

23 Alison Clark, Rosie Flewitt, Martyn Hammersley and Martin Robb (eds), *Understanding Research with Children and Young People* (SAGE Publications, 2014).

24 My thanks to the Church of England Ethics Research Panel, who performed this role for us.

25 Rebecca Nye, *Children's Spirituality: What it is and why it matters* (Church House Publishing, 2009), p. 10.

26 Jerome Berryman, *The Complete Guide to Godly Play: How to lead Godly Play sessions*, vol. 1 (Morehouse Education Resources, 2002), p. 138.

27 These three quotations are from *What Goes On Inside*, pp. 5, 3, 7.

28 William Wordsworth, 'Intimations of Immortality' from *Recollections of Early Childhood* (D Lothrop and Company, 1884).

29 However, they never sugar-coat Jesus' teaching: the dark and dangerous places of the parable of the good shepherd and the menacing presence of the wolf in John 10 are explored openly.

30 The Church of England, *Statistics for Mission 2016* (Research and Statistics, 2017): **churchofengland.org/sites/default/files/2017-10/2016statisticsformission.pdf**.

31 The General Synod of the Church of England, *Growing Faith: Churches, schools and households* (The Archbishops' Council, 2019), with links to original research data (p. 2): **churchofengland.org/sites/default/files/2019-01/GS%202121.pdf**.

32 *Painting with Numbers*, p. 21.

33 *What Goes On Inside*, p. 2.

34 David Hay and Rebecca Nye, *The Spirit of the Child*, revised edition (Jessica Kingsley Publishers, 2006). This is one of several sources that explores what spirituality in childhood looks like – including in the natural world.

35 *Painting with Numbers*, p. 43.

36 *Painting with Numbers*, p. 44.

37 *Painting with Numbers*, p. 21.

38 Church Army's Research Unit, *Messy Leavers* (Church Army, 2019): **churcharmy.org/Publisher/File.aspx?ID=224309**, p. 2.

39 Bob Jackson, 'From Sunday school to Messy Church: a new movement for our age?' in George Lings, *Messy Church Theology: Exploring the significance of Messy Church for the wider church* (BRF, 2013), p. 152.

40 *What Goes On Inside*, p. 5.

41 *Painting with Numbers*, p. 36.

42 George Lings, *A Short Intermission: How can church be expressed within the arts?*, Encounters on the Edge no. 25 (Church Army, 2005), p. 21.

43 Lings, *A Short Intermission*, p. 21.

44 Clare Watkins and Bridget Shepherd, 'The Challenge of "Fresh Expressions" to Ecclesiology: Reflections from the practice of Messy Church', *Ecclesial Practices*, 1 (1) (2014), 92–110: **doi. org/10.1163/22144471-00101005**.

45 *Painting with Numbers*, p. 15.

46 *What Goes On Inside*, pp. 7–8.

47 *Painting with Numbers*, p. 25.

48 *Painting with Numbers*, p. 29.

49 *Managing the Mess*, p. 28.

50 Nye, *Children's Spirituality*, p. 10.

51 Sara Savage and Eolene Boyd-McMillan, *The Human Face of the Church: A social psychology and pastoral theology resource for pioneer and traditional ministry* (Canterbury Press, 2007).

52 *Managing the Mess*, 'Exogenous influences', pp. 3–5.

53 *Managing the Mess*, p. 4.

54 *Managing the Mess*, p. 20.

55 *Managing the Mess*, p. 34.

56 *Managing the Mess*, p. 6.

57 *Painting with Numbers*, p. 39.

58 Jerome Berryman in Rebecca Nye (ed.), *Godly Play UK: The magazine*, No. 4 Spring (2019), p. 4: **godlyplay.uk**.

59 *Managing the Mess*, p. 7.

60 Claire Dalpra, *Small Beginnings: Church for under 5s*, Encounters on the Edge no. 31 (Church Army, 2006), p. 24, quoting Margaret Withers in an interview.

61 *Managing the Mess*, p. 5.

62 *Managing the Mess*, p. 12.

63 *Managing the Mess*, p. 15.

64 *Managing the Mess*, p. 9.

65 *Managing the Mess*, p. 30.

66 *Managing the Mess*, p. 14.
67 George Lings, *Leading Lights: Who can lead new churches?*, Encounters on the Edge, no. 9 (Church Army, 2001), pp. 10, 20.
68 *Managing the Mess*, p. 16.
69 *Managing the Mess*, p. 16.
70 Samuel Shoemaker Jr, *So I Stay Near the Door: An apologia for my life*, private pamphlet printed by Calvary Church (1958) but reprinted elsewhere under the title *So I Stand by the Door*.
71 Lings, *The Day of Small Things*, p. 18.
72 *Managing the Mess*, p. 34.
73 *Painting with Numbers*, p. 10.
74 *Painting with Numbers*, p. 39.
75 Church Army's Research Unit, *Messy Lifespan Analysis* (Church Army, 2019): **churcharmy.org/Publisher/File.aspx?ID=224310**.
76 *Painting with Numbers*, p. 19.
77 *Painting with Numbers*, p. 33.
78 *Managing the Mess*, p. 10.
79 Lucy Olofinjana and Catherine Butcher, *Talking Jesus: What can I do?* (Evangelical Alliance, Church of England and Hope, 2018): **talkingjesus.org/wp-content/uploads/2018/04/Talking-Jesus-web-short.pdf**, p. 13.
80 *Discipleship Definitions*.
81 Paul Moore, *Making Disciples in Messy Church: Growing faith in an all-age community* (BRF, 2013).
82 Andrew Roberts, *Holy Habits* (Malcom Down Publishing, 2016).
83 'Intergene-RELA-tional ministry with Terry Williams', podcast: **workxpc.com/intergene-rela-tional-ministry-with-terry-williams**.
84 **here2stay.org.au**
85 **holyhabits.org.uk**
86 Beth Barnett, 'Segregation vs sensitivity: an alternative approach to recognising and acknowledging age diversity in faith formation', blog post, 20 June 2019: **multivocality.wordpress.com/2019/06/20/segregation-vs-sensitivity-an-alternative-approach-to-recognising-and-acknowledging-age-diversity-in-faith-formation**.
87 Roberts, *Holy Habits*, p. 53.
88 Rowan Williams in Michael Ipgrave (ed.), *Scriptures in Dialogue: Christians and Muslims studying the Bible and Quran together* (Church House Publishing, 2004), p. 21.
89 Nicholas Lash, *Theology on the Way to Emmaus* (SCM, 1986), p. 45.

90 Mike Clarke, professor of zoology, La Trobe University, 27 June 2020.
91 Mike Clarke, Professor of Zoology, La Trobe University, 27 June 2020.
92 cft.vanderbilt.edu/guides-sub-pages/blooms-taxonomy
93 en.wikipedia.org/wiki/Theory_of_multiple_intelligences
94 Edward de Bono, *Six Thinking Hats* (Little, Brown and Co., 1985).
95 msn.com/en-au/news/other/urinotron-breaks-down-urine-to-be-used-as-energy/vp-AAFWVtW
96 ecobricks.org
97 Andrew Roberts and Lucy Moore, *Holy Habits in Messy Church* (BRF, 2020), p. 82.
98 Hiwi and Pat Tauroa, *Te Marae: A guide to customs and protocol* (Raupo, 2009).
99 youtu.be/tOugEQpcc_k
100 messychurch.org.uk/messygrace

Get Messy! is a four-monthly subscription resource for Messy Church leaders. Each issue contains four session outlines (one per month), including planning sheets and take-home handouts, together with information on the latest resources and events.

Get Messy!
Session material, news, stories and inspiration
for the Messy Church community
£4.75 per issue

brfonline.org.uk

LUCY MOORE and ANDREW ROBERTS

HOLY**HABITS**
IN MESSY CHURCH

DISCIPLESHIP SESSIONS FOR CHURCHES

Holy Habits meets Messy Church! The Holy Habits approach explores Luke's model of church found in Acts 2:42–47, identifies ten habits and encourages the development of a way of life formed by them. This session material has been created to help churches explore the Holy Habits in a Messy Church context and live them out in whole-life, missional discipleship.

Holy Habits in Messy Church
Discipleship sessions for churches
Lucy Moore and Andrew Roberts
978 0 85746 923 6 £8.99

brfonline.org.uk

Lucy Moore demonstrates how hospitality can be practised in Messy Church and other church contexts to promote mission and faith formation, addressing the theology of hospitality and how it can be expressed at the welcome table, the activity table, the Lord's Table, the meal table, and in the home. Also included are insights from the secular hospitality industry, how to train Messy Church teams in hospitality, audit-style questions for the reader to apply in their own context, and five complete session outlines for Messy Churches.

Messy Hospitality
Changing communities through fun, food, friendship and faith
Lucy Moore
978 0 85746 415 6 £9.99

brfonline.org.uk

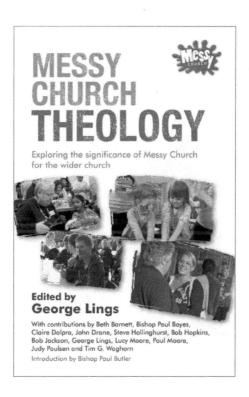

Messy Church Theology is the first title to encapsulate the theology of Messy Church. Through essays by contributors from a variety of church and academic backgrounds and case studies by Messy Church practitioners, it gathers together some of the discussions around Messy Church and assesses the impact of this ministry, placing it in the context of wider developments within the church community.

Messy Church Theology
Exploring the significance of Messy Church for the wider church
Edited by George Lings
978 0 85746 171 1 £9.99

brfonline.org.uk

Enabling all ages to grow in faith

Anna Chaplaincy
Living Faith
Messy Church
Parenting for Faith

The Bible Reading Fellowship (BRF) is a Christian charity that resources individuals and churches. Our vision is to enable people of all ages to grow in faith and understanding of the Bible and to see more people equipped to exercise their gifts in leadership and ministry.

To find out more about our ministries, visit
brf.org.uk